The Wanderer

For those who enjoy heart-wrenching teenage romance with a touch of the paranormal

DAVY TERRY

The Wanderer

2

Contents:

The Wanderer

3

First trip

Here I am alone; I am alone with myself; I don't have a brother, like or friend. Among these people, the most loving and the best friends were unanimously chosen. Carrying their enmity to the point of treachery, they cut off all the ties that united me to them, seeking what grief could most stir my sensitive soul. I could love them, even if they didn't want to; They escaped my love only by being human. At will, they are now strangers and unknown people to me; they are nothing! But what am I, separated from them and all? It is up to me to research it. But first, you need to take a look at my situation; It is also necessary to pass the word from my peers to myself.

More than fifteen years have passed since I found myself in this strange situation, and it still feels like a dream. I still have indigestion and think I'll go to sleep and join my friends when I wake up. Yes, I pass from waking to sleep, or rather from life to death, without noticing it. In the nature of things, I'm stuck in a dream where I can't choose anything. And every time I think about my current situation, I don't understand where I am.

The Wanderer

4

Ah, how could I foresee my end; Even today, I can't understand why he embraced me. I'll never change, I'll be the same, one day I'll be a monster, a poisoner, a murderer, a plaything for a mob hated by humanity, every person who passes by will say hello to me, and it's wise to assume that this generation will enjoy burying him alive in unison. will allow? Confusion and impatience drove me into a frenzy that hadn't stopped for ten years. During this time, I made mistake after mistake, folly after folly, and my carelessness gave me many tools to help me determine my destiny.

For a long time, I tried my best and fought in vain. I was resourceful, hypocritical, resourceful, and imprudent, as well as outspoken, impatient, and quick-tempered, and gave my enemies never-missed opportunities to do me new evils. Finally, seeing that my efforts and regrets were in vain, I decided to surrender without resisting fate. I was able to forget about my problem by patiently enduring the exhaustion of the disease and everything that could not be resisted in vain.

This was another factor of peace. While my cruel enemies were devising other tricks to tempt me, they forgot one, which was to continually renew the effect of their cruelty, and strike a new blow each time. If they had shown me the ability to leave a glimmer of hope, that hope might still hold me in its arms,

The Wanderer

distract me, and condemn me to new sorrows with my unfulfilled expectations. However, they finished without using all the tools they had; They left me nothing and deprived themselves of everything. Their slander, mockery, shame and humiliation that suffocate me cannot increase or decrease; nor can they strengthen it, and I cannot escape it. They worked so hard to bring my wretch to the limit that all human power, even all the tricks of hell, could do nothing to it. And the pain of the body comforts me, that it increases the pain, and saves me from sighing when I groan; My body's disintegration stops my heart from breaking. Now everything is done; What else am I afraid of them? Because they can't make me worse, they can't put me in a new fear. Worry and fear, I have escaped from these two troubles; this is also a benefit. Real challenges affect me less; I endure hardships, but I am not afraid. They take many forms in my hasty imagination; expands, grows; waiting for them is more dangerous than meeting them; Fear is worse than being shot. But when they do, they lose their imagination and find their original quality. And I see these difficulties easier than I thought, and I find relief in the midst of pain. And so, I get rid of all new worries and sorrows of despair, I draw easier every day because I get used to a situation that nothing can aggravate, and as time goes on, as I become less sensitive, it becomes more difficult to arouse it. My adversaries have done me this favor, having exhausted all the means of incalculable enmity; they

The Wanderer

could not keep me under their power. Now I can have fun with them too.

Less than two months have passed, and my heart is at peace again. For a long time, I was not afraid of anything; but I still had hope. Then, this hope, sometimes fed and sometimes deceived, became a car of various desires and thoughts that turned me upside down. A sad and at the same time unexpected event finally extinguished this dim light of hope in my heart and decided my fate on earth once and for all. From that day on, I surrendered unconditionally and attained peace.

As soon as I began to see the whole order against me, I well understood that I could not win the people over to my side until I survived; In fact, this peace, which could not be mutual, was no longer useful.

From now on, even if people turn to me, they will not be able to find me. My dealings with them would be meaningless and a burden to me because of the favor they instilled in me; I find happiness in solitude that I cannot find in living with them; People took away all the pleasures of social life from my heart. I cannot feel that pleasure at this age; the work is done. From now on I will be indifferent to everything that comes from them, whether they do good or bad; No matter what they do, my opponents can't do anything for me.

The Wanderer

7

But I still hope for the future, that a conscientious generation will examine the judgments of the present generation on me, the behavior it deems appropriate, expose the deception of those who govern it, and finally see me as a human being. I am a. It was this hope that led me to write down my "Stories" and to a thousand foolish attempts to leave them for posterity. This hope for the distant future brought (me) back to the beat of my heart when I was still searching for a righteous heart; Those hopes that I want to push me have turned me into a toy of people today. I told you in my "Talks" that I relied on expectations. However, I was wrong. I realized in my last hour that I was wrong and managed to find a break from my frustration and relax before it was time. That hiatus began at the time I am talking about; There are reasons to think that it will not be cut anymore.

Not a day passes without measuring my error in the hope that the public will turn to me with new ideas; here it was wrong to expect the influence of time; Because those who have grown up, as well as for me, are led by regular guides of communities who hold grudges against my personality. Individuals die, but communities do not. The same passions and habits live in them; Their enmity is as immortal as the demon that consumes it, so they continue to do the same thing. Even if all my enemies are dead, the doctors and the preachers of the churches will live. Even if my enemies remain only as this doctor and

The Wanderer

8

orator, I believe that they will not leave me alone in death, just as they did not leave me alone when I was alive. I really resent the doctors, maybe they will adjust in time; but these ecclesiastics, semi-monk orators, whom I love and respect, and whom I trust so much, will always remain steadfast. My guilt was born of their cruelty; It is a crime for a people who do not forgive their honor and constantly try to feed and fuel their enmity to remain at least as enemies as themselves.

It's all over for me. Here they cannot do me any good or bad. I have nothing in this world to hope for or to fear; I am comfortable at the bottom of the abyss; a man who will die wretched and as immoral as God himself.

From now on everything outside of me is foreign to me. I have no relatives or brothers left on earth. I felt like I fell from another planet. If I look around and pick one thing, it breaks my heart, everything I see about me is something that moves or hurts me. Let's leave the painful issues that cause unnecessary grief. I am alone until I die because I have lost comfort, hope, and silence from myself, I do not want to work with anyone but myself. It is in this situation that I continue to examine what I once called "confessions," ruthlessly but sincerely. I spend my last days studying myself and preparing in advance the account I will

The Wanderer

9

soon give. Let me enjoy talking to my soul. This spirit is something that people cannot separate from me. It wouldn't be too much if I could get over them, sort out my tendencies, and correct the remaining evils in them. Although there was no use for me in this world, I spent my last days in vain. I regret that I often forget about my daily travels. I write down the things I remember, and every time I read them, I get new pleasure. When I think of what reward my heart deserves, I forget my troubles, those who have afflicted me, and the insults I have suffered.

These pages will be just a random diary of my fantasies. They have a lot to say about me, because a person who thinks in solitude is naturally concerned with himself. However, it includes other thoughts that come to my mind while traveling. I say what comes to mind, and the less space between them, the less thoughts about the day before and the day after. However, these allow me to get to know myself and my character better by expressing the feelings and thoughts that my mind constantly feeds on in the strange situation I find myself in. Thus, the following pages may be regarded as a supplement to "my confessions"; but I do not call them "confessions"; because there is nothing to say in this way. My heart was purified in the fire of suffering; No matter how carefully I examine it, I can find no reprehensible character in it. What else can I accept after the love of the world is torn from that heart? I neither praise nor

The Wanderer

slander myself; I am now nobody among the people; I cannot be anything because I have nothing to do with them. I could not do any good so that it would not turn into evil; I cannot act without harming myself or others; abstinence took the form of a duty that I would fulfill as best I could. But despite this immobility and unemployment of my body, my soul is still moving; it still gives rise to thoughts and feelings, its inner life seems to grow with the cessation of all earthly, material interest. My body is now only an obstacle, a burden for me, and I try to get rid of it as much as possible.

Such an interesting situation, of course, requires analysis and description. This is where I devoted my last free time to this review. To achieve this, it must be organized and methodical; but this is beyond my power; in fact, recounting the changes in my soul and their phases distracts me from my purpose. I do the same procedure that astronomers do every day to understand the weather: I apply a manometer to my soul, and this well-controlled, repeated procedure produces results as reliable as the astronomers'. conclusions. But I will not promote this enterprise to them. Instead of trying to turn the process into a method, I'm going to record it. For another purpose I will try like Montaigne; for if he writes his essays for others, I do not write my imagination for myself alone. If, as I grow older and nearer my departure, I remain in a state of anticipation, reading them will remind me

The Wanderer

of the joy of writing and double my life by recreating the past. Regardless of the people, I will continue to enjoy social life, I will continue to live in my old condition as if I was living with my younger peers.

I was writing my first "Confessions" and "Words" with the thought that I would save them from the hungry hands of my enemies and pass them on to future generations if I could. I do not feel the same anxiety as I write this piece of mine; I know I don't have to; My desire for people to know me better is now extinguished, and I have nothing in my heart but a profound indifference to what will end up with my true writings, my documents of innocence, perhaps all to-day. Tracking my activities and behavior, these pages are of interest and I no longer care that they are hacked, deleted or changed. I will not hide what I write and I will not show it to anyone. By seizing them while I am alive, they will not be able to take away from me the pleasure of writing, nor the memory of what they contain, of my thoughts, of which they will be the only work and source. with me. If I had known that I would not defy my fortunes, and that I had made up my mind to-day, as soon as my downfalls began, all the terrible tricks of men, with all their efforts, would have been ineffective against me, and they could have done nothing. spoil my comfort by their deceptions, as they cannot spoil mine by their present success: let them freely enjoy the abominable

The Wanderer

state in which I am; They cannot prevent me from enjoying my innocence and ending my life in peace.

The Wanderer

13
Second visit

Thinking to describe my usual state of mind in the most mysterious state a man can fall into, I found the easiest and safest way to accomplish this endeavor, simply to write down my wanderings and wandering dreams as they were. These hours of solitude and reflection are the only moments when I can truly say that I am completely free from extraneous thoughts and that I am what nature intended me to be.

I quickly realized that I was too late to implement this idea. My imagination, which has lost its vitality, does not burn as before in the presence of the object which had set it in motion. Delusions of fantasy make me less intoxicated. There is more memory than creation in the present objects of my imagination. All of my habits have gone into a warm swoon. The spirit of life is slowly fading away from me. My soul is out of a useless vessel, and I deserve it if there is no hope of the realization of the situation I hope for. And so, to see myself before I am completely submerged, I must return to the time when I was gradually nourished by its essence and accustomed to find its nourishment within myself, when I had given up hope on earth and found no food to nourish my heart...

This path, which I discovered too late, was so fruitful that I forgot all about it. My habit of contradicting

The Wanderer

14

myself eventually made me insensitive to my problems. I learned through experience that the source of happiness is within us, and that it is not in the hands of people to make the happy unhappy. For four or five years, I have felt the inner pleasure of loving and gentle people leaving this world. This ecstasy, this ecstasy in which I wandered alone, was the pleasure of those who treated me cruelly: without them I could neither find nor see my inner treasures. How can I keep track of all this wealth? Wanting to remember such a sweet fantasy, instead of describing it, I went back into them. This is a state of incomprehensibility when the memory returns to itself and is not felt. I really thought about interrupting the flow of my thoughts, and diverting them for a while, especially in connection with that unexpected event, and writing an appendix to "My Necks" on my next travels.

On Thursday, the 24th of November, 1776, after dinner, I followed the great avenues to the rue Chemin-Vert, and ascended the Miniloan range, and there, by a narrow path between meadow and vineyard, I passed through the beautiful countryside which separates them. these two villages to Caranna; Then I passed through the same meadow, but on a different road. Taking a break from time to time, I looked at the grass on the lawn, saw beautiful places, and wandered here and there with pleasure and interest. I saw two grasses, which I rarely see around

The Wanderer

15

Paris, but which are abundant in that meadow. One was 'Picris hyracoids' from the compound genus and the other was 'Bupleurum falcate' from the canopy. I really enjoyed finding these and kept me entertained for a long time. At last, this led me to discover a very rare plant, especially at high altitudes, 'Cirsium aquaticum', which I found in my book and in my herbarium, notwithstanding the accident of the same day.

After examining many more herbs, each of which I knew very well, and whose appearance still pleased me, I finally gave up these little observations, and surrendered myself to a more pleasant and, I think, effect. He made me one of them. The visa expired a few days ago; the people from the city were returning, and the villagers were leaving the countryside to return to their villages from winter work. The grass is still green with its leaves torn off, but the fields are deserted because the people have retreated; The whole place took on the appearance of the coming winter. The sweet and sad effect of that face was so similar to my age and happiness... Although my soul was still full of lively feelings, and my mind was now decorated with a few flowers full of pain, I finally saw myself. innocent and unhappy life. As I began to feel the cold air of old age for being alone, my withering imagination ceased to entertain the lonely universe with images adapted to my heart. "What crime have I committed in this world?" I sighed. I was saying. I was

The Wanderer

16

born to live; I will die without living. I don't think it's my fault, and even if I can't offer my creator the good that I wasn't given the opportunity to do, I can at least give my thwarted good intentions, my pure but ineffective feelings, and my infinite tolerance for human conflicts. Humiliation? These thoughts moved me; my soul, from my youth; Ever since I was banished from human society as an adult, I watched their attacks in a corner of solitude that I would retreat to for the rest of my life. I fondly remembered all the love, blind interest, and comforting thoughts that had nourished my soul for several years, and I tried to express them with deep pleasure, as in life. . The afternoon was spent in such peaceful thoughts, and I was returning from a day's excursion very contented, when the incident I am about to describe pulled me out of the hottest stage of my fancy.

At six o'clock I descended the slope of the Maimonian, and reached the opposite side of the Galant Jardinière, when several men stopped suddenly in front of me; I realized that a large dog speeding after a passing car could not stop or change direction when it saw me; I immediately thought of jumping into the air so that the dog wouldn't roll me to the ground and he wouldn't pass under me. This thought, which I did not even have time to implement, flashed through my mind shortly before the accident. I heard neither fall nor fall until I came to.

The Wanderer

17

When I came to, it was like night. Three or four young men, who remembered me in their arms, told me what had happened: The dog could not control its speed, threw itself between my legs, and hit me on the head with all its might; My upper jaw, bearing all the weight of my body, hit the protruding stone, and it was low, so that my head to my feet touched the ground, and I fell very badly. The horses would have passed me if the driver leading the dog owners had not stopped immediately.

This is what I learned from those who carried me when I came to. My mood that December was so strange that I can't help but mention it here.

It was night. First, I saw the sky; then some stars and green... This first feeling was very sweet to me. I was still feeling myself because of this influence. It's coming to life and I thought I filled everything I saw with my weakness. I couldn't remember anything, I just lived as I was. he cannot distinguish who I am; I didn't know who I was or where I was. I felt no pain, no fear, no anxiety. I looked at my blood flowing like a stream, I didn't think it was mine. I felt such a pleasant peace in my whole being that, when I remember it, I do not think I can enjoy it as humanly known. They asked me where I lived; I couldn't say. I asked where I was. They said I was in Upper Bourne, but it was as if they said "At the Atlas Mountains"; at

The Wanderer

the end they had to ask me in which country, city and quarter I live; It didn't help them understand who I was. I couldn't remember where I lived or my name until I left and reached the main streets of Paris. A master, whom I did not know, but who was kind enough to walk with me a little, realized that my house was far away, and advised me to take a cart from the Temple quarter. Although I was spitting up a lot of blood, I did not feel the wound or pain, and I walked easily. But the cold made me shiver and my bad teeth clenched together. As for the area around the Temple, I was a comfortable walker, so walking was more convenient than freezing to death in one of the cars. I walked the half-hour between the Temple and the rue Paltrier without difficulty, avoiding crowds and cars, and it was the same as before the accident; I opened the secret lock they had put on the street door, climbed the stairs in the dark, and finally got into my room without meeting with anything but disaster. The fact that my wife screamed at me showed that I was in a worse situation than I thought. At night I am not aware of my condition; What they saw the next day was this: my upper lip was split from the inside to my nose; my skin protected it from the outside and prevented it from tearing completely; four of my upper teeth were stuck in my jaw, and the part of my face covering that area was swollen and damaged; the thumb of my right hand was broken, and my left hand was severely injured; My left arm was injured and my left knee was swollen. This knee

The Wanderer

19

hurt so much that I couldn't even bend it... However, despite shaking so much, I didn't have a single tooth broken; This is a miracle considering the extent of my accident.

Here are the details of the accident. In a day or two the story spread all over Paris; it had changed so much that it was impossible to understand the truth. I should have known this would happen. But the innuendos and allusions to this story, the strange details, the funny behavior that pretends to be unspoken, eventually took on a mysterious quality that troubled me. I have always hated dark things; no matter how many years they have surrounded me, they evoke the same hatred. Among all these curious circumstances of this period, I will mention one which is sufficient to comment on the others.

Mr. X, with whom I had no relation, sent me his servant to inquire after my health, and offered me some assistance, which I did not think would be of any use in the circumstances, as assured me, for instance. The secretary urged me to accept these suggestions, and went so far as to say that if I did not believe him, I should write directly to Mr. X. Both this curiosity and the secrecy with which he was shown it made me suspicious; There was a secret beneath it that I could never understand. All this was enough to make me fear disaster and the wave of fire that would follow.

The Wanderer

20

Indulging in anxious and sad delusions, I resolved what was going on around me not as the composure of a man of no account, but as wandering from the fire.

There was another incident that completely blew my mind. Madame X has been following me for years for reasons I can't understand. His gifts of pleasure and aimless frequent visits, which could not be called natural, were telling me something, but I could not understand. He told me about a novel he wanted to write to present to the Queen. I also expressed my opinion about women who write articles. And he intimated that his thoughts were directed to returning to his former high state, and that he should be shown favors in this way, to which I could not answer. After that, because he could not get close to the queen, he said that he would present his book to the readers. It's past time to give advice he doesn't want and won't listen to anyway. He said he wanted to show me his work before it was published, but I asked him not to, and he refused.

One day, while recovering from an accident, he sent me his book in print and hardcover. I saw sentences that warmly praised me in the introduction; however, these words made a very bad impression on me, so hesitant and contrived. I sensed the crude flattery of

The Wanderer

21

the headline; sincerely inconsistent; My heart will never be deceived in this respect.

A few days later, Madame X came to visit with her daughter, and reported that she was making a fuss over the writing in her book; It seems that this note did not catch my attention while scratching the novel; After my guest left, I read it again, and looking at what was written, I understood the reasons for the author's praise of his travels and the praise in the preface. I saw that the purpose of all this was to make the writing more expensive for the readers, and to make me feel guilty in terms of its publication.

I could neither stop this noise nor prevent its consequences... All I had to do was acknowledge the unnecessary and noisy visits of Mrs. X and her daughter and not prolong the rumor. Here is my letter to the woman on this matter:

— Mme. Rousseau, who does not welcome any writer into her house, thanks X for his kindness and begs her not to be honored by his visits any longer.

His reply, though polite in form, was written like all the letters I receive on such occasions. I thrust a savage dagger into his sensitive heart; His feelings for me were so warm and sincere that he would have

The Wanderer

died because of the breakup of our relationship...
Here, honesty and openness are considered to kill
people; It is enough not to be fake and treacherous
like them in order to appear evil and cruel to people.
Now I was on the street; I have been to the Tuileries
several times. But as I wandered around and was
surprised by the people I met, I realized that there
was another news about me that I didn't know...
Finally, I heard that I died after an accident. The news
spread so quickly that fifteen days before I knew it, I
was pronounced dead in the palace. Moreover, as I
learned from my letter, the newspaper "Le Courrier
Dairen" while writing this happy event took the
opportunity to announce the ceremony prepared for
my memory after his death.

Added to this news was another strange story that I
happened to know about, which I don't understand in
detail: they started collecting money to publish my
doodles found in my house. After my death I realized
that many articles that I had written were kept ready;
For the idea that I might have the idea of suppressing
my authentic writings, which are to be discovered, is a
folly which no sane man would do after fifteen years'
experience.

overlapping and many others joined in and threatened
my dream once more, I thought I had decided. These
darkness's, which constantly surrounded me, also caused

The Wanderer

me to fear them. Tired of describing and interpreting them, I began to unravel the mystery that had led me to a state of incomprehension. The result of all my efforts was to confirm my former thoughts, for the fate of me and my reputation was decided by the present generation, and I could not be saved no matter what I did; After all, I can't leave anything to future generations so that it doesn't fall into the hands of those who have an interest in destroying it.

But this time I went further. A confluence of many unrelated events; As if fate had made it, my most cruel enemies were lucky. It seemed so special to me that they were all people who ruled the state, led the community, and were dignified people who could not secretly attract me and participate in cooperation, it was impossible to interpret. as a coincidence. If there was one person or any incident against me that did not agree to this agreement, it would immediately become null and void. But for the purpose of these people; Desire, fate, results, changes helped; This wonderful cooperation was what God wanted to achieve. My observations of yesterday and to-day have so confirmed this opinion, that I cannot understand the reason why I look upon circumstances which I believe to be the result of the wickedness of men, as one of the commandments of God.

This thought not only calms me, but also leads me to surrender to fate. I will not go as far as Saint Augustine, who agreed to be in hell if God willed; My

The Wanderer

acceptance of fate was not motivated by myself, but sincere and I think more worthy of the perfect man I long for.

God is just. He wants me to shoot him, but he knows it's not my fault. This is where my faith comes from; My heart and mind declare that I am not deceived. Good luck and let people do what they want; Let's learn to shoot without making a sound; Everything eventually dissolves into the order of the world: sooner or later it will be my turn.

The Wanderer

25
Third visit

I am growing old by reading.When Solon was old, he often repeated this line. It makes sense that I can use it for myself when I get old; but the experience and knowledge that life has given me in twenty years is very sad; I prefer ignorance. Misfortune is certainly the greatest teacher; however, this teacher sells his lecture very dearly and is not worth paying for its usefulness. Moreover, the opportunity to benefit from such a delayed lesson end. Youth, mind training; Old age is also a practical time. I admit that experience always teaches something; but how old we are is measured by time. What's the point of understanding how to live when it's time to die? Of what use is the truth discovered so late and painfully to my destiny and to the passions of others who wrote it? Getting to know people better has helped me better hear the pain they put me through; moreover, I could not stop myself from falling, even though I saw one trap after another. I wish I could remain in the silly and sweet confidence that has made me the toy of my rowdy friends for years, and I can't feel anything, even if it's abuse! Although I was deceived and victimized by them, I thought they loved me, and I was convinced that they were sincere in that love. These beautiful fantasies have been destroyed. The sad truth that time and reason have revealed to me has shown me that I am doomed, that I am hopeless and that there is no other way but submission. Therefore, all the events of

The Wanderer

26

my age and current age will not benefit either today or tomorrow.

We leave the battlefield we entered at birth with death. What is the benefit of knowing how to use our race car better at the end of its life? All we have to do is figure out how to get out of this. If there is one thing an old man can learn, it is to learn to die; but, on the contrary, it was the least done at my age; nothing but death is considered. The elderly is more devoted to life than children; die harder than young people. Because they work all their lives for this world and in the end, they see that they work for nothing. When they migrate, they leave all their possessions and the fruits of their efforts. When they were alive, they didn't think that they would have nothing to take with them when they died. I told myself before the time was up. but my thoughts are inconclusive, not because I fail to think them in time. Throwing myself into the world at a young age, I learned through my own experience that I was not made to live in it, that I would not have the life that my heart desired. Thus, my ardent imagination, without asking people for the happiness that I could not find among them, as if fleeing from a foreign land, jumped to the far reaches of my new life and settled on a comfortable foundation. I could take a break. This feeling, learned from my childhood and reinforced by the devastation that later filled my life, has always led me, more than others, to explore my existence, what I don't have, and

The Wanderer

27

its purpose. I have seen many people philosophize far more intelligently than I; but their philosophy seemed alien to them. Because they wanted to be more knowledgeable than others, they would study the world and understand how it was originally built; but they had nothing but interest in examining the machine upon which they had accidentally stumbled. If they had tried to learn about the creation of man, they would have been able to speak of it wisely; not to understand themselves. Many have liked to write a book because it might be well received; they worked to educate others, not to educate themselves. If their books are criticized after publication, they don't care about the content of their books, regardless of whether others have received these criticisms, whether they are guilty or not. I wanted to learn, not to teach others, but to know myself; There is nothing I have learned while living among men, and even on an island where I am condemned to live for the rest of my life, there is nothing I do not aspire to. What we want to do depends on what we have to believe; In all matters unrelated to the essential needs of nature, our behavior is dominated by our thoughts. As I pondered how to manage my life based on this rule I had always accepted, I found solace in my inability to be resourceful on earth, searching for the essence, the essence of life. understand this purpose.

I was born in a family that respected morals and religious rules, I was brought up by a wise and

The Wanderer

religious priest, and I grew up with beliefs and principles that I have not forgotten since my youth. I was left alone as a child, tasted love, lost hope, felt need, and became a Catholic; but I have always remained a Christian; Soon, following my habit, I became deeply devoted to my new religion. Mrs. de Warens' teaching and examples to me made this commitment even stronger. I felt the loneliness of the village where I spent the best time of my youth, my passion for books with all my soul; He nurtured my innate capacity for love at that young age and gave me a devotion close to Fenelon's. Contemplating in the corner of solitude, studying nature, observing the universe makes a lonely person always jump to things, to the creator, to search for the purpose of everything he sees, the reason of everything he hears with sweet concern. When fate threw me back into the storm of the world, I found nothing to distract my heart. The sweet memory of my leisure led me to a neglect of high duties, and of the means at hand to lead to riches; He hated them. In the ambivalence of my complex desires, I had little hope and little profit; But even in the days that I lived with hope, I felt that even if I got everything I thought of, I could not find the happiness that my heart longed for without knowing what it was. Thus, even before the destruction that beset me with the world, everything was urging me to get rid of the interests of this world. I hesitated between poverty and wealth, wisdom and depravity, I had no evil thoughts in my heart, I got rid

The Wanderer

of bad habits, I did not rely on my mind, I lived in confusion, I forgot my duty, I forgot my duty, and I reached the age of forty. offensive, but often fail to foresee them. Since I was young, I considered this age to be the last stage of success and all my claims, and when I reached this age, I decided to live every day without trying, no matter what the situation. Don't think about the future, get out of that situation. When the time came, I made my decision without difficulty. At this time, although my life would be more or less improved, I gave up with real joy, far from sadness. After ridding myself of these delusions and vain hopes, I abandoned myself to indifference and prudence, which is my chief pleasure and tendency. I also gave up dressing up; I bear no sword, no watch, no white stockings, no gilded and false hair. On my head would be an ordinary wig, plain and coarse; moreover, I had taken away from my heart the passions and desires that valued the things I said goodbye to. I quit my non-professional job at the time and started writing for my long-time hobby.

I did not give up on organizing my life. Having come to a further and necessary decision in the eyes of others, determined to cut him off at once, to see him die, I put my life in order and entered into my account.

There was a great change in my soul; I had discovered another spiritual world; I realized the absurdity of

The Wanderer

people's unconscious judgments, I did not yet know that I would fall prey to it; hearing his voice, I needed a blessing other than literary fame, which I loathed; I was looking for a safer path than the one I had spent the better half of my life on; All of this has led me to a point I have long considered necessary. So, thinking about it, I didn't focus on anything I could do to get to the end.

My separation from the world, the pleasure of solitude that I have not left since then, begins on this date. The work I intend to write can only be written in complete solitude; it required a long and calm reflection that was impossible in the tumult of the world. It led me to a different life. I loved life; After giving in against my will for only a short time, I happily rejoined when I got the chance. So much so that I have found that the people who condemned me to a life of solitude in order to make me unhappy served my happiness more than I did.

I started my work with an effort that aligned with the value I gave and the need I felt. At that time I lived with the ancient philosophers. Instead of dispelling my doubts and indecisions, they shook my belief that I had reached the points I most wanted to know. Because these dogmatic people, ardent defenders of "Atheism", could not make me think differently on any subject. Not liking to fight, and having no talent for

The Wanderer

fighting, I defended myself freely; but I never accepted their sad beliefs; My objection to these conservative men, that each of them had his own purpose, was the main cause of their enmity.

They threatened me if they could not deceive me. The evidence they adduced did not convince me, but made me shudder; I couldn't find a suitable answer, but I felt it was necessary. I blamed myself for incompetence rather than delusion, and my heart answered them better than my mind.

, when I don't even believe that the ideas they spread and impose on others are theirs. It prevents them from learning what they believe. Is it possible to seek favors from party leaders? Their philosophy is other peoples, and I need philosophy. Let us seek with all our might while we have time, so that we may acquire a principle of unchanging conduct throughout life... Here is maturity I have reached the age of understanding, the highest stage of understanding. I can no longer dominate my habits, I can't do what I can today; let us take advantage of this favorable opportunity: it will improve my material conditions, at least intellectually and spiritually. Allow me to make a decisive decision, and after careful consideration, I will be there for the rest of my life."

The Wanderer

32

I worked on this project slowly and intermittently with great care and effort. I knew very well that my life and destiny depended on it. In performing it, I was at first thrown into such confusion, difficulty, darkness, contradiction, and entanglement, that I could not understand, and had no foundation, but wished to obey the caution followed by all, and wish not to depart. everything is in its place and do not try in vain. But even this prudence was alien to me, and I could not reach him, and to guide him was like seeking a port in a stormy sea, where even beacons could not show.

But I resisted; I showed courage for the first time in my life; Under the influence of this courage, I was able to withstand the terrible end that awaited me without knowing it. After perhaps the most fervent and most earnest inquiry that any man ever made, I resolved to feel to death what I ought to feel; I believe that even if I am wrong, the results I have achieved will not at least expose my error as a crime; because I used all my strength to prevent such a crime. In fact, there is no doubt that the baseless judgments of childhood and the secret desires of my heart seem more attractive to me. It is hard not to believe something so fervently requested; And no one doubts that the acceptance or rejection of judgments in the Hereafter will be a factor of hope and fear, the belief that is often cultivated by people. I admit that all this may spoil the happiness of contemplation; but he could not corrupt

The Wanderer

33

the purity of my heart; because I was afraid of being wrong about everything. If it's all about managing this life, I should know that I can make the most of it without delay (cheating). But what I feared most was to endanger my soul in attaining eternity under the pretense of partaking of worldly blessings, which in this state I could not appreciate.

Again, I confess that I have always hesitated and doubted because of my inability to solve the difficulties that our philosophers have set forth. But at last, I resolved to come to a decision in matters over which the human mind could not dominate, and everywhere faced with unsolvable mysteries and unanswered questions, and in each question, I chose the most fundamental and self-assured opinion. I have not addressed the strong evidence to the contrary and the conflicting evidence that I cannot resolve and cannot refute. Only charlatans can make shorthand judgments on these matters; The important thing is to come to a unique opinion with a mature mind. However, if we are wrong, it is not our fault. It is an unbreakable foundation of trust and security.

The result of my incessant research is more or less the same as what I wrote in the "Profession de foie du Victoire Savoyard"; it is such a work that it is despised and defiled by men of the present day; If people have

The Wanderer

34

common sense and good intentions, they can make a revolution.

Since then, I have considered the principles I have adopted after long and deep reflection to be the invariable rules of my faith and conduct; I stopped paying attention to conflicting thoughts that I couldn't understand, and thoughts that didn't occur to me before. These thoughts troubled me from time to time, but they did not sway me. I used to repeat to myself, 'All this is nothing but a metaphysical detour, after the passions which my mind accepts and my heart approves, and when I am silenced, they are nothing before the principles to which they stamp the seal of sincere assent. Is it possible that a sect that is beyond the reach of the human mind, so carefully thought out, reasonable, and without any other problem, that has come and gained power at the whim of my thinking, can be upset for some reason? The question I cannot answer? In the spiritual order, whose principles and order I have discovered through my research, I find the help I need to bear the sufferings of my life. In any other faith I would live and die without hope; I would be the unhappiest of people. Therefore, regardless of luck and people, it is best to cling to the faith that is enough to make me happy.

I wonder if these thoughts and the conclusions I draw from them have been instilled by God to prepare for

The Wanderer

35

and endure my end. How would I be in this incredible state of being judged for the rest of my life, with no place to escape from, no place to escape from, no place to escape from, no hope of reparation for their abominable condition? Have you placed me in this world, on the right side of the hope of justice, if I am the victim of a terrible fate that no man has seen? Thinking that people will show me only admiration and sympathy with the calmness of my intelligence, while my open and pure heart was given to my friends and brothers, the traitors silently surrounded me with a hellish trap. I fell to the most terrible, and at the same time to a proud soul, unexpected disasters, dragged down to the ground without knowing why or by whom, sank into the abyss of humiliation, and stumbled at first when darkness enveloped my surroundings. I sensed sinister intentions; If I hadn't gathered my strength beforehand to withstand these blows, I wouldn't have been able to pull myself together after the sudden collapse.

As the years rolled by, I finally came to my senses; I realized the value of these powers that I saved for the bad days. When I had decided all the questions that I could judge, and compared my position with my principles, I found that I valued men's foolish thoughts and the little incidents of a short life more than they did; Again, I see that life is a notebook of exams, so it doesn't matter if these exams are one way or the other; enough for the expected results to come

The Wanderer

out of them. Thus, as those trials grow, intensify and multiply, the more the power of endurance is developed, the more useful it will be. There is no pain that does not diminish the strength of those who wait for their reward; My belief in this award is the result of my previous thoughts.

During the many abuses which I have suffered on every side, there is not an interval of anxiety and doubt which disturbs my hope and comfort. Almost crushed by the weight of fate, some basic thoughts that I could not understand were gathering in my mind and preparing to destroy me forever. Often there was also new evidence that agreed with what I had previously thought. Then, as if my heart was suffocating, "Oh!" I thought to myself, "If I find that the consolations, I think are vain dreams, who will save me from despair? What can I hope for in fancies that can comfort no one else? In the sentiments that feed me alone, the present generation finds only error and vanity, the truth is in my contrary opinion, He sees that I am sincere in this belief, that I do not fully believe that I myself will find insurmountable difficulties in it, no matter how strong my will is. , but even if I cannot overcome them, my blood will not change.. Am I the only one among the people who have attained wisdom, am I the only enlightened person? is it enough to make sure that everything is in its proper place? I believe good in appearances that do not correspond to others, and if my heart did not

The Wanderer

support my mind, would I even consider the imagination? Pardon me, but I am nothing more than a victim of delusion."

How often have I despaired in those moments of doubt and arrogance! If this situation lasted a month, I would be done. But these crises, though frequent, were brief; Even today, when I can't get rid of them, they pass quickly without disturbing my peace! In other words, just as a feather falling into a stream cannot disrupt the flow of water, these small worries affect my soul less. I have come to understand that dealing with the points I have already decided upon presupposes that I have new realities and new powers of thought; As this was impossible, at a mature age of mind, and my quiet life having no other interest than the search for truth, I was exhausted by despair, and could not prefer the thoughts that sought to destroy me forever. feelings that come after thinking. Today, when my heart is suffering from such pain, my mind is tired, my soul is trembling, my mind is dizzy from the terrible secrets that surround me, and all my habits are weakened by the influence of old age and worries, shall I give up the funds? of the consolation which, though I am unworthy, is ready to compensate me for the sufferings I have suffered; Shall I hug your fallen side and be utterly miserable, with a solid part of my sanity left? Are not. I am neither wiser nor wiser than the day when I have decided all these high affairs. I knew then the troubles

The Wanderer

38

I now regret; but they could not stop me; If the unthinkable happens, these are the absurdities of a deceptive metaphysics that cannot negate the eternal truths that have been accepted by all ages, all sages, and all nations, and which are indelibly written in the human breast. Thinking of these things, I know that the mind of man, limited by the senses, cannot sufficiently comprehend them; so, I stayed with what I could understand and didn't go beyond that. This decision I once made was wise; I clung to it with the contentment of my mind and heart. Why should I give up, there are so many reasons not to be attached to it at the moment? What is the risk of not giving up? What do I gain by opting out? Shall I join the sect of those who treated me cruelly and adopt their morals? Although that rootless and fruitless morality never entered the mind or heart of anyone, it is clearly shown in books or brilliant performances of the theater; Or do I accept the secret and abusive morality that forms an inner sect of other confidants, dominates their actions, and has been so skillfully applied to me? This morality, which is purely "evil", is useless for defense. What would it profit me if my enemies overthrew me? Only my innocence gives me strength in my ruin; Wouldn't I be unhappy if I replaced it with evil? Can I do evil and reach my enemies? Even when I grow up, what evil can I do that will save me from my doom? It humiliated me and I would have nothing more. This is how he thinks about deceitful thoughts; I have been able to stand firm in

The Wanderer

39

my convictions without obscure proofs, and without difficulties which, perhaps, the human mind could not solve. And as for my own intellect, it was so comfortable, that in the firmest condition I could secure it, no extraneous thought, old or new, could disturb it or me. Due to the tiredness of my head, I forgot my convictions and thoughts on which my principles were based, but I will no longer forget the judgments I made with the consent of my mind and consciousness, and I will no longer adhere to them.

Let all the philosophers come and attack me; their time and energy will be wasted. Whatever I choose, I will stay with what I choose.

So not only am I comfortable, but I find in him the hope and comfort I need for my situation. Such complete, unceasing, and sad solitude, the bitter hostility which the present generation has shown and always felt, the insults which I have always seen fit, cannot but despair me; Hopes, constant pauses sometimes hurt my soul. And I must remember my old resolutions, for I cannot engage in mental exercise to calm myself; My faith is renewed when I remember the care and sincerity, I showed in making those decisions. So, I reject any new thought as the result of an empty and dangerous delusion that only serves to destroy my comfort.

The Wanderer

40

Confined thus in the narrow frame of my old learning, I could not, like Solon, find the happiness of learning as I grew older; From now on, I have to guard myself against the desire to learn things I don't know. But though I have no useful knowledge, yet I have much to gain by virtue of my condition. Behold, the time has come to enrich my soul with the benefits it brings with it, when that soul, freed from the cage that surrounds and blinds it, sees the truth in all its nakedness and feels the pain of knowledge. our foreign scientists are proud. The time spent trying to achieve that knowledge in this life will be wasted. The only wealth that you can take with you, increase every day, and not be afraid to depreciate in death, is patience, moderation, submission, right direction and fair justice. This is the only and useful subject that has given me the remaining years of my old age. If I can walk away from life on the mend, it's not better than the day I was born (indeed it's impossible), but better!

The Wanderer

41
Fourth visit

Of the books I still occasionally read, Plutarch's works are the most interesting and useful to me. It was the first thing I read as a child; the last thing I want to read when I'm old; I can say that I am the only writer who has taken lessons. One day I was reading one of his books on morality, "How to Gain Advantage from Enemies." That same day, while editing pamphlets sent to me by some authors, I came across one of the notebooks of the Reverend R***. In front of it is written: "Vitamin Vero impendent." Knowing what kind of words people like him use, I was not fooled this time either, and understood that he was mocking behind the veil of subtlety. But what was the point? What could be the purpose of this mockery? What did I do to him for this mockery? In order to profit by Plutarch's lecture, I decided to make an excursion the next day, after checking my lie; When I began this work, I reconsidered my earlier belief that the phrase "know thyself" in the Temple of Delphi was not as easily followed a principle as I thought in My Confessions. The next day, when I set out to put this idea into practice, the first thing that came to my mind was a lie that I told when I was young, and which still hurts me in my old age. This lie, which constitutes a crime by itself, takes on the character of a more dangerous crime in its consequences, which I have not yet learned, but greatly exaggerate his remorse. But, considering the mood I've been talking about, those

The Wanderer

lies were simply the result of overindulgence; Far from the intention of harming the woman who is his victim, I swear, the moment I lie out of pride, I am ready to give my life so that he does not harm anyone but myself. It was such a crisis of unconsciousness that I can only explain it, my shyness thwarted all the desires of my heart.

The indelible regret that I remembered this terrible experience awakened in me a hatred against the lie that would protect me from it for the rest of my life. When I lay down my principle, I am very worthy of it; but R.

And I am proud of my love for the truth; I was amazed at how many things he made up and claimed to be true, even when I sacrificed my confidence, my interest, and this truth with a fairness I never saw in any of my peers.

What surprises me the most is that I don't feel any deep regret when I remember these lies. I, the one who hates lies more than anything else, the one who endures sufferings that can be avoided by lying and the one who has repented of lies for fifty years; How did I tell a needless, unnecessary lie, and I don't regret telling it? My crimes have never brought me any stigma; the moral instinct always guided me, my conscience never left honesty; Even if this conscience

The Wanderer

is destroyed by following my interests, how can a man retain his justice in cases where his passions are seized, but lose it in matters of less importance? I saw that the correctness of my judgment about myself depended on the solution of that question; After studying it carefully, I managed to explain it as follows:

I read in a philosophy book that lying means hiding the truth to be told. By this definition, failure to state an unspeakable truth is not a lie. But if a person who is not satisfied with not being able to tell that truth says the opposite, is he lying or is he lying? Again, if the definition is used, it is impossible to understand who is a liar. After all, he certainly cheated a person who did not owe money by giving him fake money, but he did not steal.

Two important questions arise here; The first is: We owe others the truth, when and how should we tell the truth? Second: Are there times when you naively deceive others? I am well aware that in a society where the most conservative morals are considered impossible, the second question is cut to the right in books that come free to the author. Let's put aside the authoritative people who argue with each other and reject each other's opinions, and try to solve these issues with our own ideas:

The Wanderer

44

General, i.e., abstract truth, the most precious of blessings. It is as if a person cannot see anything without the eye of the mind; thanks to it, people learn how to behave no matter what, do what is necessary, and move towards their main goal. The truth that a person reaches is not always correct; something that is often wrong and almost always useless to anyone. There is not much, perhaps, that is useful to every man's happiness, and that he ought to know in this respect; but not much, his right and property, he seeks everywhere; Depriving him of it is also the worst form of theft, because these things are among the common benefits that do not deprive the giver by giving them to others.

Benefits in education and everyday life

As for truths that are not true, how can we say a good thing that is not actually a good thing; And since property is based on interest, there can be no profit where there is no property. The soil may be good, though barren; because at least it was built upon; but the truth or falsity of an absurd phenomenon that has no meaning for anyone does not affect anyone. Nothing is superfluous in the spiritual and material spheres. What is not useful is not a right; You have to work to calculate it. Thus, the truth which we call right belongs to justice; To apply the concept of truth to things whose existence or knowledge is

The Wanderer

meaningless to anyone is to abhor the concept. Therefore, even, if possible, a truth deprived of any utility cannot create a right, and therefore one who conceals it is not lying.

But are there facts that are useless to anyone? This is a topic that needs further discussion; I will talk about that soon. For now, let's move on to the second issue.

It is one thing not to tell the truth, another to tell a lie; but the same result can be obtained from both, because the result is the same, and therefore there is no other way. The truth is nobody's business, and the opposite is not true either; It follows that, in the same cases, a person who deceives by telling the opposite of the truth is no more guilty than lying without telling the truth; for ignorance is worse than being mistaken about useless truths; It is no different from not knowing the color of the sand on the seabed or not believing that the sand is white or red. If it is unjust to harm others, is it unjust not to harm anyone?

But, in short, these things have no practical use, if they are pre-lit, they can be used very well in any situation. If the obligation to tell the truth is based on its benefit, how do I resolve that benefit? Often the interests of one cause harm to another; self-interest is almost always at odds with the common good. How to behave in such a situation? Should we sacrifice the interests

The Wanderer

of those who are not related to us for the interests of those with whom we are related? Doesn't he tell the truth that benefits one and harms the other? Should we measure what we say only by public interest or by all-encompassing justice? Do I know enough about the subject to apply what I know fairly? there is more; In considering what we owe to others, have I properly considered what we owe to ourselves, to the one truth? If I don't hurt someone while cheating, does that mean I won't hurt myself?

Isn't it unfair enough to be perfect?

Let us not part with truth, justice is truth, in our actions, in the anti-constitutional arguments upon which our faith depends, lies are always injustice, error is fraud. Telling the truth, no matter what, is a crime, because we don't tell our truth. escape; but this is considered a shortcut; does not solve. The truth of the matter is this: Is it obligatory to always tell the truth, not to always tell the truth? Moreover (a question whose answer I think is in the negative) is to distinguish situations in which telling the truth is absolutely necessary from situations in which it is necessary to change without unjustly concealing or lying. I know that such situations really exist.

But where to get such a rule; How can one prove that this is an infallible rule? I have always benefited from

The Wanderer

47

solving all such complex spiritual issues with my conscience rather than my mind. Moral instinct has never deceived me; He kept his purity in my heart, which I can always trust; although it does not interfere with some of my actions, it always dominates my mind; Here I make harsh judgments about myself that will be given in the hereafter. Judging people based on the impact of their words is not judging them properly. These effects are not always predictable and vary depending on the context and time in which the words are used. Moreover, only the owner knows whether it is good or bad. In order for telling the truth not to be considered a lie, there must be no intent to deceive. Since it is not clear that the intention to deceive is motivated by a desire to do evil, it can also have a completely opposite purpose. The absence of the will to do evil is not enough to make a lie harmless; moreover, we must believe that the mistake we made will not harm them or others. Such an opinion is rare, so the lie is almost never innocent. Lying for one's own benefit or for someone else's benefit is dishonesty; If it is a lie told to harm and break, it is the most indecent of lies. Lying without thinking of benefit or harm to oneself or someone else is not a lie, it is a form of lying game.

Myths based on moral issues do not emphasize the lies that cover the truth because they spread useful truths that are easy and pleasant for everyone to

The Wanderer

understand; Anyone who tells a myth simply as a myth is not lying in any sense.

There are also empty myths, as in many stories and novels, which have no lesson to teach, and are merely entertaining. Morally useless, their value is determined by those who invented them; if they are asserted as fact, they must be considered false; but who hesitated or condemned such a lie? For example, if there is a moral issue in "Temple of Nidd", that issue is ignored by many sensitive (sexual) details.

What did the author do to cover them with a veil of purity; He claimed that his work was translated from Greek and convincingly explained how he found the book to convince readers of its authenticity. If it's not a complete lie, then let them determine what is. Even if the truth of the matter is like this, no one has come forward to put a lie on the face of the author.

That this is a joke, that the author did not intend to deceive anyone and that no one was deceived by him; moreover, it can be remembered that everyone knows that the author himself translated the work written from Greek; But what's the point? My reply was that such a joke would be foolish childishness if it were without purpose; a liar told a lie even if he did not convince anyone; In addition to those who understand what they read, there are ordinary and

The Wanderer

simple readers who believe that the ancient writing speaks in a pure tone, and they will not hesitate to drink from the ancient cup, and will not drink the poison from their own bowl. the time.

Whether such distinctions are in the books or not, there are men of good will who will not consent to anything they cannot bear: For it is as much a lie (though less severe) to say a false thing for our own advantage.) as a word spoken to the detriment of another. To give an opportunity to the unworthy is to violate the order of justice; Actions that demand admiration or condemnation from ourselves or others, and anything that impresses people in one way or another, is a lie. Here is the exact scope of the work; but everything that does not concern justice, even if it is wrong, is a myth: I will say frankly that those who reject those myths have a more conservative conscience than mine.

Lies told in order to serve are true lies; for to assert them on behalf of others or ourselves is as unjust as asserting them against ourselves.

A person who speaks for or against the truth is lying when it comes to the real person. And if we are talking about a "fantasy" person, a person who evaluates the morality or wrongness of his inventions and whose judgments are not correct, whatever he says is not a

The Wanderer

50

lie, unless he is lying with facts. , he is speaking in terms of moral truth.

I have often seen such people called "realists" in public life. The truth observed in empty and meaningless words; It is limited to counting each place, each day, and each person correctly, not inventing anything, not exaggerating events. They care about strict realism in their stories, unless their own interests are at stake; but when it's their turn to talk about something that touches their personality, they paint it every color to show their side of things. Even if it is his job, if he refrains from telling lies with his own mouth, he skillfully tells others and forces them to accept them without making excuses for them. Wisdom: "Truth... After all, honesty!" says.

What I call "correct" is very impressive. It does not interest him in trifles that someone else counts so much, and he does not hesitate to amuse his friends with stories that do not touch anyone and do not lead to unjust judgments; but he does not use the tongue or the pen, he does not use even the slightest word that is against the truth and the truth, that harms anyone. In a normal conversation, it is right even if he does not tell the truth, even if it is against his own interests. True, he does not try to deceive anyone, on the contrary, he is equally committed to the truth that supports and opposes him; He does not seek to

The Wanderer

51

dominate for his own benefit or to the detriment of his enemies. The difference between a righteous person and another is that a person of society is firmly attached to the truth that does not require any self-sacrifice; can't go any further; and the person I think serves only when he has to sacrifice the truth.

You say, how can the true love I have for him be combined with such carelessness? Is this contagious love fake? No, it is pure and clean; however, as a representative of justice, he does not want to be false, even if it is often "mythical". For him, the words truth and justice are synonymous; He uses both at random: The sacred truth he prays for is not made up of meaningless stories and unnecessary words, but rather what each person has a right to each person, in each situation, for example, good or bad, honor or crime, approval or condemnation. Since he does not wish harm on anyone, he is not false to himself either, because he does not accept anything that does not belong to him. His envy is self-respect; This is the only virtue he cannot give up, and he knows that it is harmful to gain the respect of others at the expense of virtue. Thus, he does not hesitate to lie about small things that can harm or benefit someone or himself; but he protects himself and others from going astray as much as he can in matters of truth and justice. For him, no other lie is a lie.

The Wanderer

52

If "The Temple of Grid" is a useful work, it is a tale translated from the Greek as an innocent fiction; but if this act is dangerous, it should be a myth and he should be punished.

These were the principles of my conscience regarding lies and truth. While my thoughts were still mine, my heart followed them indifferently; moral instinct was also put into practice. The treacherous lie of which poor Marion was the victim made me so sorry, that it has saved me all my life, not only from such lies, but from any lie which injures the interest or honor of others.

In this, as in other things, my habits, principles, or rather my habits, had a great influence on me; for I have not done any of my actions according to the rules; or the heavens of my creation, I am not bound by any rule. I did not lie for my own gain, just as I did not lie willingly; but I have often lied because I was ashamed or about matters that were not important and only interested me: for example, when I had to make up words when my head was out of order. but that he is not a liar when telling a tale, i.e. I make sure that truth and justice are not touched. Instead of the truth of the events in them, I want to squeeze moral truth and learn useful lessons from human passions, in a word, "feelings"; but this requires a facility to speak with intelligible rapidity which I do not possess.

The Wanderer

53

Since speech is more urgent than thought, I speak without thinking, which has resulted in me saying a lot of nonsense that doesn't sit well with my mind.

Due to the irrepressible impulse of my Creator, my shyness leads me to tell lies against my will in unexpected situations. Poor Marion's memory trace, though it prevents lies that would hurt others, doesn't just affect those who helped keep me out of harm's way; but my conscience does not take such pleasant interference as the objectors.

If I could drop the lie that saved me, and immediately, without humiliating myself, put it in its place, I would be afraid without a second thought; but the shame of self-blame still hinders him; I regret my crime, but I cannot undo the damage it caused. Let me give you another example of how I lied not out of interest or pride or envy or malice, but simply out of senseless awkwardness, unnecessary shyness.

On several occasions, Mr. E invited me and my wife to dinner with Mr. B at Mrs. X's restaurant (against my habit). A woman in a restaurant and her two daughters ate with us. While eating, one of the married and pregnant girls looked me in the eye and suddenly asked if I had a child. I blushed, I said that such happiness is not enough for me. He smiled and

The Wanderer

54

looked around. There was nothing here to darken my eyes.

It is evident that the answer I gave was not one I would give even if I did not want to; for, considering the mood of those around me, nothing I could say could change their minds. Even my response was negative and he did his best to enjoy watching me lie. But I wasn't kind enough to understand that. Two minutes later, my answer came automatically: "That's one of those awkward questions a young woman can't ask an unmarried old man." By speaking like this, I would not lie, everyone would like me and I would be a lesson to them. But I could not; I said the unsaid, not the unsaid. It is evident that it was neither my mind nor my will that inspired me with this answer; this answer was given only because of my surprise. Once upon a time I would not have gotten into such a mess, I would have said it more clearly; because I had no doubt that factors would be felt to forgive them. However, I was surprised by the evil eyes; Every time I was unhappy, my shyness increased, and I lied just because I was ashamed.

I never felt such a strong hatred of lying as when I wrote my Confessions; for the desire and opportunity to lie (if I had any inclination to lie) was most evident when I was writing this work. But, hiding nothing from me, but with my understanding, which I had not

The Wanderer

yet understood, and perhaps because I hated to imitate, I turned instead to falsehood. In other words, I blamed myself for excessive conservatism. And my conscience tells me that one day I will be judged less harshly than others. Yes, I can proudly say that in this work I have brought good intentions and true love before anyone else has dared. I realized that their good points outweighed their bad points, so I found it useful to tell them all, so I told them all.

I was wrong; I said now; but when describing the situations surrounding them rather than events. This type of lie is more a form of my imagination than a desire. Moreover, it is wrong to falsify these additions; because none of them is false. When I was writing "Confessions", I was an old man, I was tired of the pleasures of life that I had, and I experienced its emptiness. I was writing my book without any documents, just from memory. My memory, on the other hand, was often unable to help me or to revive my recollections incompletely; I miss this. I made up for this deficiency with my imagination, but I made sure that they did not contradict each other. I liked to dwell on the happy moments of my life, I decorated them with beautiful things that I drew from longing. Sometimes I also added a non-specific beauty to the truth; but I did not exchange this truth for a lie to cover up my sins or to look good.

The Wanderer

56

Although sometimes I involuntarily showed myself from the side and not from the front, I hid my bad sides, but I compensated for such concealment with other concealments, and because of them, I hid more of the good than the bad. Perhaps this strangeness of my character is hard to believe; But the fact that I don't believe it doesn't change the fact that I'm telling the truth. I spoke of the bad with all the ugliness, but I avoided making the good beautiful; Being on my side, I didn't even touch on it, because at that time I was in a position to praise myself for writing "Monandry". When I talked about my youth, I didn't tell stories that would point to my good points, unless I told them. I remember two stories from my childhood; These were not in my mind when I was writing my book, but I dismissed them for the reasons I have already mentioned.

I spent Sundays at the house of one of my cousins, Mr. Faze, the husband of the publisher. One day, I was in the place where the fabrics were laid, and I was looking at the casting molds. I loved the way they glowed, I wanted to touch it with my hand and ran my fingers over the roller. In the meantime, my brother-in-law's son turned the steering wheel, two of my fingers were pinched, and two of my fingernails were pulled out, and I cried in pain. Fuzzy immediately stopped the wheel, but my fingernails were stuck to the roller. My fingers were bleeding. Surprised, Faze ran up and hugged her, saying that if I don't keep

The Wanderer

57

quiet, I will fall. Forgetting my pain, I thought of him and became silent; We ran to the faucet, washed my hands, and stopped the bleeding. He begged me not to tell this story to his father; I made a promise to him, and I kept it so firmly that twenty years later, no one knows why my fingers are cramping. I was in bed for three weeks; I could not use my hands for two months; I told those who asked that my hand was crushed by a stone.

However, my accident had some consequences at that time: Since it was the time when the city's youth went to military training; I had to wear a uniform and practice with my three children of my age in the department of our district. So, lying in bed, I was sad to hear my three friends walking past the door playing the Rota.

My other story is similar to this one; but this passed after a few years.

I was playing with a friend of mine named Pins in Disaster at Plain Palais. As I was playing, I had a quarrel with him over a difference of opinion; If we were fighting, he hit me on the head with a hammer, saying that if he hit me harder, my brain would explode. I fell to the ground as I was. Never in my life have I seen the poor boy rush to my blood. He thought he killed me. He jumped on me, hugged me, cried and

The Wanderer

58

screamed. I cried like him. Finally, trying to stop the bleeding that was still flowing, seeing that even with both of us wrapped in a scarf, it could not be stopped, so he took me to his mother, who lived nearby. The poor woman fainted at the sight of my condition; but he gathered himself, and washed and bandaged my wound, and applied lilies dipped in the spirit commonly used in our country to the wounds. The tears of the woman and her son touched me so much that I thought of one as my mother and the other as my brother until I left and forgot the story for a long time.

I did not tell anyone about my accidents. I had about a hundred of them, but I didn't even name them, because I didn't want to talk about the goodness of my character. When I spoke against the truth I knew, I found it hurt no one, or I had pains to speak, or pleasure to write; but I did not intend to harm myself or anyone. If anyone can read "My Confessions" with an objective eye, he will realize that the confessions in it are to be considered more serious than the great crimes, and that they are much more serious than the explanation of the great crimes I have committed. Not to say I didn't, but to say it's a shame.

All this shows that my choice of the path of righteousness is based more on my love of truth than on my sense of rightness; Indeed, in practice I

The Wanderer

followed the moral path of my conscience, not abstract notions of right and wrong. I have told the tale many times; but I lied very little.

Adhering to this principle, although I gave many weapons to others, I did no harm to anyone, and I did not give myself more privilege than I deserved. In my opinion, the property of truth is realized only in this way. In other words, truth is a concept that serves neither good nor evil.

But such thoroughness does not satisfy me as much as I think that I am innocent. As I carefully weigh what I owe to others, have I carefully considered what I owe to myself? If we need to be fair to others, we must be realistic about ourselves. It is a debt of respect that a mature man must pay for his dignity. I guess I did it wrong because I couldn't think of anything to say; for it is absolutely wrong to humiliate myself under the pretense of entertaining someone else. And in the pleasure of writing, I made the great mistake of embellishing real events with fanciful ones; because to embellish reality with myth is to change it.

But if there's one thing that's unforgivable, it's the principle I've chosen. This principle compelled me to be truer than others; it was not enough to sacrifice my interests and affections for him; I also had to sacrifice my shyness. Showing the courage to be right every

The Wanderer

60

time, at every opportunity; There should be no lies, fabrications, or myths that come from a mouth or pen that is fully committed to the truth. I must think of them in mastering that lofty principle, which I had to remember when I carried it. Never has hypocrisy induced me to lie; they always arose from my weakness; but they still don't count as apologies. A weak spirit only protects us from being rude; but to be moral the argument requires no less courage.

Here, if the honorable R. I think it's time to put these forwards; but perhaps I did not miss an opportunity to explain my mistake and sharpen my ability to distinguish between good and bad. In this and similar works, the words of Solon may be applied to people of all ages; being smart, honest and humble and not trying to reap anything from yourself.

There is no time to learn (even from our enemy).

The Wanderer

Fifth Trip

None of the places I've lived (and I've lived in beautiful places!) have made me so happy and longing for the island of Saint-Pierre on Lake Bien. Even in Switzerland they know little about this little island called Motte in Neuchâtel. As far as I know, no traveler has mentioned it. However, it is a very attractive island that will make those who like to be alone happy; (Perhaps due to fate, although I am the only one who suffers from loneliness, I think that there are people around me who do not see them and enjoy loneliness.)

The shores of Lake Bien are wilder and more romantic than those of Geneva; for though the rocks and woods are much nearer to the water than there, they do not mar the beauty of the coast. There are few cultivated fields, vineyards, special dwellings and houses, but there is a lot of greenery and shady trees. Fortunately, there are no roads where cars can pass, so there are not many passengers; but it is very beautiful for those who love nature, listen only to the sound of the eagle and the waters that fall from the mountains. In this beautiful, almost circular basin, there are two small islands, one of which is about two and a half kilometers, a residential area and its soil is cultivated; the other was left alone; In order to

The Wanderer

62

remove the debris created by the storm waves on this large island, the earth will be removed from it and one day it will disappear. Here the essence of the week is always used for the benefit of the strong.

This island is the property of the Bern Hospital, and there is only one house, which is also the property of that hospital, and under that large, beautiful and comfortable roof, lives the publican with his family and servants. This man has poultry, birds and fish. The soil and appearance of this small island is so different that it lends itself to a variety of cultivations. There are fields, vineyards, forests, trees, in the shade of various trees, surrounded by various trees and pastures where rivers can be seen. The high point of the island is planted with two rows of trees in the form of a terrace, in the middle of which is a beautiful hall, where on Sunday's people from the neighboring shores gather and dance. in vintage. It was on this island that I took refuge after being stoned to death in MO tiers. I found this place so beautiful, so suitable to me, that I resolved to remain here till I died; My only fear was this: the first thought I heard about those who wanted to deport me to England was the fear that they would not agree with my decision. Moreover, I was very worried and wanted to live here for the rest of my life.

The Wanderer

63

They only allowed me to stay on the island for two months; but here I would spend two years or two centuries, sit down to the end of the world, and live with my companion, with no one to be seen but his wife and servants, and the tax collector, who were very good people. I needed this. I remember those two months as the happiest time of my life; I couldn't want anything else; I was content to live there and I was very happy.

What happiness is this; What pleasure did it bring? By describing my life there, I advise my contemporaries to discover its secret. Of all the pleasures I desired, the most important was that precious "ferniest" (*), and when I really sat down, it was the pleasant and necessary pursuit of one who did nothing.

I could not go out without permission, I could not be seen, I could not see anyone but those around me, and the result was the hope that they would gladly allow me to stay in this place that embraced me. I hope to live better than before, thinking that I have a lot of time to settle here, I did not take any initiative in this regard. At one time I brought my housekeeper, my books, my belongings one by one to this place, alone and naked; I didn't open the boxes, I left them as they were, and I lived as if I was living in a house that I would live in for the rest of my life, in a guest house that I would leave tomorrow. The environment I

The Wanderer

found here was so comfortable that no matter what routine I set up, I would break it. My greatest pleasure was to put my books in a trunk and not have a writing kit. When I was forced to reply to useless letters, I would use the taxman's pen set and return it immediately, saying that I would never use it again. Instead of filling my room with those empty papers and books, I was filling it with flowers and herbs; By now, after the doctor's inoculation at Livernois, I soon fell into routine botany. I wanted fun, not work, so I was looking for entertainment to be lazy. I have tried to mention "Flora periinsular" to describe all the flora of the island. I did not forget any of them, I used to describe them in detail that I will remember for the rest of my life. It is said that a German wrote a book about lemon peel; I could write a book about meadow moss; I didn't want a blade of grass or a small plant to go unpictured. For this noble purpose, every morning after breakfast together, with a magnifying glass and the book "The Nature of Systems" under my arm, I wandered about a part of the island (I divided the island into small squares to travel according to the seasons.) The structure and structure of plants and nothing but the pleasure and joy of observing the then new efficacy of the male and female elements in fruition. As he studied the reproductive characteristics of plants found everywhere, he seemed happy; I was hoping to find some that were less common. The splitting of the long achenes (etamins) of Honeybabagillar species, the flexibility of

The Wanderer

65

nettles and sticky grasses, the bursting of a small sheath in the green wood of the squid flower nut, thousands of tiny fertilization scenes left me. He was happy and asked everyone, "Have you read Habakkuk?" he asked. As La Fontaine had asked, I asked the man in front of me if he had seen the horns of the chef's house. Two or three hours later, when it was raining, at noon, I was coming home with the bundles. By noon the publican, his wife and

Teresa and I visited their caretakers, mostly to help them. Bertines who visited me used to watch me climb big trees and jump over the rope while filling a bag of nuts. I was resting comfortably, eating and enjoying the physical exercise I did in the morning. But when there was plenty of food and good weather called me to go out, I would not wait any longer, get up from the table, get into a boat, and if the water was calm, I would go to the middle of the lake. , lying on a boat, staring at the sky, floating on the water for hours; that December I would have sunk into a thousand mixed but sweet dreams; they were more beautiful than the most beautiful of the so-called pleasures of life, if not of any particular theme. As the sun set, reminding me that it was time to head home, I knew I was too far from the island and would do my best to get there before dark. Sometimes, instead of opening the water, I preferred to go down to the green shore of the island; How many times the clearness and cool shadows of these places have

The Wanderer

66

tempted me to take a dip; but, in most of my boat trips, I went from the big island to the little island, and spent half the day there; sometimes I wandered among willows, black maples, pyrites, and various plants; They were very convenient for keeping rabbits that could be raised harmless and harmless. I told these things to the taxman; he also had male and female rabbits brought from Neuchâtel. The man's wife and Teresa, one of his sisters, and I took the animals and placed them on a small island; they began to multiply before I left; If they survived the winter cold, they increased a lot. The founding of this little rabbit society was a celebration. Maybe the Argo sailor guide who drove my friends and bunnies from the big island to the small island didn't like me either. I was proud to say that the tax collector's wife, who was afraid of water, and her seasick wife, got into the boat with me without hesitation and was not afraid at all.

When the lake was too rough for boating, I used to gather grass here on the island in the afternoon; sometimes he sits in lonely and beautiful corners and plunges into my dreams; Sometimes I settle on one of the dominant parts of the landscape, or on one of the hills, with fertile and rich plains, shores and a magnificent view of the lake, surrounded on one side by the nearby mountains, and on the other by the vast mountains.

The Wanderer

67

In the evening, I would come down from the hills of the island and rest in a hiding place among the bushes on the shore of the lake. There, the roar of the waves and the lapping of the water captivated my attention and prevented any further agitation in my soul; he made me dream insatiably. I would stay there until nightfall. The beautiful and incessant murmur of the water coming and going (a whisper that filled my ears at times) was enough to replace the fantasy that blocked my anxious thoughts and give me the pleasure of feeling that I was living without trouble. thinking. Every now and then, I was inspired by the sight of these waters and thought about the indecisiveness of our lives. But those faint impressions were lost in the constant motion that rocked my boat.

After dinner, if the weather was good, we would look at the lake and feel cool. He rests a little in the palace; laughs and talks; We used to sing the old songs, of course, better than the current ones, and finally, we were happy with that day and went to sleep hoping that the next day would be the same.

This is how I spent my time on the island, aside from the unexpected boring guests. Although fifteen years have passed, when I remember this sweet life, I feel a longing; What caused me to yearn so relentlessly and intensely?

The Wanderer

68

In my long and ever-changing life, I have found that the most enjoyable times are not the fondest and touching memories I have. These brief ecstasies and moments of ecstasy—more or less flaming—are rare occasions at any stage of life. They are very rare and temporary to create a mood; The happiness I long for is an ordinary but lasting state of being that brings happiness in its length and duration, even if it contains no life in itself, rather than the minutes that come and go.

Everything on Earth is in a constant state of flux. Nothing has a fixed form, and our love for things that are visible naturally passes or changes with them. These loves that are behind us or ahead of us sometimes remind us of a lost past and sometimes herald a failed future; There is nothing hard in them to close our hearts. Therefore, we can only live on earth with temporary pleasures; I don't really believe in the sweetness of eternal happiness. Even in our deepest pleasures, there are times when we say, "I wish the moment would never end." How can we call happiness a temporary state of mind that leaves emptiness and anxiety in our hearts, yearning for the past and yearning for the future?

The spirit can endure completely, can collect itself completely without remembering the past and reaching out for the future; can lose track of time; If

The Wanderer

69

there is a state of existence in which the pleasures of poverty, the pleasures and sorrows, the desires and fears of poverty are not needed, then as long as this state continues, everyone will seek a mature and perfect happiness that leaves no void within them. he can say that he has received a soul that needs to be filled, rather than a flawed, poor, and relative happiness found in the comforts of life . Here I have experienced this mood many times on the island of Saint-Pierre, where I dream of lying on a boat drifting with the current, or sitting on the shore of a rippling lake, or leaning on the beautiful water's edge.

Why enjoy this situation? I think, not from outside, other than ourselves, other than our life; If man lives, he is as self-sufficient as God. The infinite sense of life is a precious sense of contentment and peace; Beautiful and sweet for those who know how to get rid of sensual and material feelings that tempt us and spoil the taste of life. But most people who are full of incessant passions are not aware of this state of mind; or they know so little that they cannot taste it. Moreover, those who want this sweet ecstasy to abhor the ever-changing life they need are wrong in today's conditions. But the unfortunate man, who is ostracized from society and can do nothing for himself or for others on earth, finds a kind of happiness that wealth and the like cannot take away.

The Wanderer

70

It is clear that this happiness is not felt by everyone, in every situation. The heart should be calm, no passion should disturb the peace; There is a condition that feeling is the help of spirit and environment; any vacation or emergency situation; but it requires a uniform and continuous, moderate and even movement. Still life is only unconscious sleep. If the movement is too strong or continuous, it will wake up; It reminds us of our surroundings, breaks the spell of imagination, separates us from ourselves, and puts us back into trouble as if we are under the yoke of fate and people. A certain peace brings sorrow; it is a kind of death; then you need the help of a happy imagination; This help naturally grows into something that God does not spare. The movement that does not come from outside will be in us. Rest is incomplete, but more pleasant; because light and sweet thoughts do not shake the core of the soul, but seem to crawl only on its surface. Those thoughts are enough to remind us of ourselves and forget our troubles. Such fancies can give pleasure where no one can prevent them; Whether in the Bastille or in a dungeon, where nothing caught my eye, I often fancied myself indulged in sweet fancies.

To be honest, it is naturally isolated from the world, where everything seems to me like pretty pictures, where the few people who live there form an intimate community without my constant attention, and if I can behave myself or do. On a desolate and fertile island,

The Wanderer

where I could laze about all day long, unhindered and unchallenged, he could reach better, more pleasant dreams. This opportunity was well suited to phantasmagoria, who knew that even among the most repulsive things he could feed himself with beautiful fancies, listening to himself at will with the help of things that really touched his sensibilities. After a long and pleasant reverie, seeing the greenery, flowers, and birds around me, and gazing upon the fairy-tale shores surrounded by the clear waters, I associated all these lovely scenes with my imagination, and slowly came to my senses. my feeling, I would not know where fantasy and reality are divided; because everything helps to make my life sweeter in this beautiful place. If I could start that life again; If I could end my life in this dear island, and see no one to remind me of the ruin I have enjoyed for so many years, and never leave again; I would forget these people there, but it seems they will not forget me; But if they can't come and bother me, what's the point? Freed from all the worldly passions of social life, my soul ascends above this air and mingles in advance with the immortal soul with which it hopes to join. I know people will try to keep me out of such a good shelter, they don't want to leave. But they cannot stop me from visiting the wings of my imagination every day and enjoying myself as if I were still there. The most enjoyable thing I can do there is dream as I please. Am I not fantasizing that I am there? I will go further: I will add an immutable, abstract imagination,

The Wanderer

72

the descriptions that bring it to life. Although I can't understand the meaning of those descriptions when I'm passed out, the more vivid my imaginations, the more colorful they seem. Moreover, I shall be more than I have been in them; Sadly, as the imagination loses its fire, this feeling grows heavier and shorter. What a pity; the least we see of it is when it's almost time to break free from our skin cage!

The Wanderer

Sixth trip

If we look carefully, we don't have automatic actions in our hearts that we can't find a reason for.

Yesterday I was crossing the new street to pick hay in the Gentilly area on the banks of the Beaver stream, and I turned right as I approached the Enter gate. I went into the countryside, on the way to Fontainebleau, into the hills overlooking the river. It really didn't make any sense that I was going in that direction; but, remembering that I had seen it several times without realizing it, I couldn't stop laughing after I searched and understood the reason.

Every day in summer there is a woman and a very cute son who comes to a corner of the street outside the Ener Gate and sells edible roots and small bread; but the child is lame; Leaning on crutches, he sweetly begs passers-by. We met this little man. As soon as he sees me, he will come and tell me, I would give what I have to give. At first, I liked him very much, and gladly gave him a few coins; I enjoyed it a little; I always used to talk to him because I found his speech very sweet. However, this pleasure gradually acquired the status of a habit; In the end, it became an assignment for me. However, the fact that the boy started calling me by my name to show that he knew him, and that I had to listen to them independently began to annoy

The Wanderer

me. Therefore, after that day, I did not pass there, I walked along winding roads.

Until now, I didn't notice it, I found it while thinking. This observation reminded me of many others which proved that I was ignorant of the real and true motives of my actions. I know and feel that doing good is the truest happiness that a human heart can feel. But it has been a long time since I was allowed to attain this happiness; It is impossible for those who have experienced my wretched fortune to find an opportunity to do good. Whatever goodness they have, is only a trick to lure me into the trap they want to lure me into, because those who have the upper hand over my destiny are careful to make everything appear to me to be false and deceitful. I know this; Now I know that the only good thing from me is to refrain from any behavior and actions knowingly and knowingly for fear of doing evil.

But there were happy moments when I followed my heart and made others happy. It is a matter of note to me, that when I tasted that pleasure, I found it sweetest of all; it was a true, passionate and pure character; No emotion in me denied him. However, I was saddened to find that my good works had imposed many responsibilities on me; thus his pleasure was diminished; While I enjoyed these missions at first, they ended up being excruciatingly

The Wanderer

75

boring. During my short and blessed tenure, I was approached by many people, none of whom were fired. However, because of these good deeds that upset my heart, I would have to do a lot of work that I did not expect and could not avoid. For those I ministered to, these first favors were a prelude to what was to follow; Every unfortunate person who tied me to him with the good he received from me , left this good free for those who need it in the future by my own will. Such sweet pleasures quickly turned into heavy obligations. However, when I lived as a stranger, I did not hear about the burden of these chains. But when, through my writings, my character began to be known to all (a delusion which is difficult, but more than paid for by my destructions), I became the man sought by all suffering men, or the so-called unfortunate adventurers. They tried to deceive me, pretending to have a great reputation and capture me in one way or another.. I came out. Then I realized that all our natural inclinations, including goodness, change their nature and become harmful as before when they are accepted into society without hesitation. All these bitter experiences gradually changed my inclinations, and, on the contrary, at last closed their borders; they have taught me not to blindly follow my own good will, which makes the evil of our favors less palatable.

But I don't get caught up in these stories; for by making me think, they made me know myself, and

The Wanderer

many times revealed the true causes of my conduct, when I was in a state of fancy. That I may not be compelled to enjoy doing good, that I may be free; I realized that it is enough for it to take the form of an obligation in order to be deprived of the pleasure of doing good. Therefore, the sweetest pleasures become burdens of necessity. I think, as I wrote in "Emil", if I lived in the country of the Turks, I would be a very bad husband at the hour when the mourners called me to perform my husbandly duties.

It changed my long-held opinion of my moral character; For virtue is not doing good by following our desires, but rather overcoming those inclinations when required by duty and fulfilling the requirements of duty that I can do less than others. I was naturally sensitive and compassionate, enjoying being human and being useful, sympathizing with weak wills, and inspiring generosity. (But if I had an interest in my heart; if I were a strong man, I would be the best and most beloved of men; it would be enough for me to use the opportunity of revenge to extinguish the desire for revenge. I seek justice even against my own interests, but I am just for the sake of those I love I couldn't bear to be, my heart is my duty. When there was a conflict between us, there was little victory. I often protested, but it was always impossible to act against my will. Whether people dictate or demand duty and necessity, my heart is silent. when I stand, I am silent. the destruction that threatens me, but

The Wanderer

instead of preventing it, I allow it to come. Sometimes I start by trying, but the trying soon wears me down, I can't go on. Then I can't do it. .

There's more: Obligation and my desire go hand in hand, but if it's too much pressure, it turns into hatred. That's why the kindness I did without knowing, when asked, carries a burden. I do my good deeds of my own free will without expecting anything in return; but if the person who has this good wishes for the good to continue as his due, if he forces me to do a good thing until I die, as the law says, pleasure will be replaced by boredom. . Then whatever I do is not from good intentions, but from weakness and excessive shamelessness; So I scold myself.

I know that there is a sacred covenant between the benefactor and the benefactor; it is a kind of partnership between the two, more intimate than other people; If the benefactor accepts gratitude implicitly, the benefactor continues to be worthy of his attention, shows his good intentions, and undertakes to keep the good to the best of his ability or as long as he is asked. These are clear and precise terms; are the natural results of the relationship between them. If a person refuses to provide the requested help for the first time, he has the right to appeal to the helper; but after helping once, he does not accept the second help, destroys the hope that

The Wanderer

was the cause of his birth, deceives and hopes unnecessarily. In this second refusal there is more cruelty and rudeness than the first; but there is also an effect of emptiness, which the heart loves and does not yield easily. I fulfill my duty in paying the debt; I feel good when I donate. Now, the satisfaction of doing one's duty is a habit which is only the result of an acquaintance with decency; Direct creations cannot rise so high.

After such painful experiences, I often avoided even the best things I could have done, afraid of the distractions of my work duties, and accustomed to seeing from a distance the results of my expected instinctive behavior. without thinking about it. I didn't always have this fear; On the contrary, many times I saw that those who received my help in my youth were bound by a feeling of gratitude, not self-interest, just as they were bound by my kindness to others. . However, this, like so many other things, changed when my destruction began ; Since then I have lived among people of a generation quite different from my own, and my feeling for others has been affected by the changes I have seen in them. The people I met from both generations, so different from each other, seemed to fit both. At first they were honest and open, but after they changed, they became like everyone else. The change of time was enough for people to change. How can I feel this way about those who were born upside down? I cannot hate them because I

The Wanderer

cannot hate them: but I cannot hide what I do not like; They already deserved it.

Perhaps I have changed too much without realizing it; Who can put up with the situation I'm in? I believe that after twenty years of experience, the good tendencies that nature has created in my heart have turned against me and others, and now I look upon the good that is expected of me as a trap. For me and under it lies evil. I know that whatever may be the effect of the work I am about to see, it will not fail to carry as good a virtue; but though his virtue was infinite, his pleasure was gone. after the enthusiasm of pleasure is gone, apathy and coldness appear in me; My mind joins the rebellion of my pride, and instead of inner warmth and pleasure, I'm left alone, I don't want it, I'm tired.

There are certain calamities that lift and strengthen our spirits; some will slaughter him: behold, I pass by. If the leaven of my soul were a little quenched, it would stir it up; but (on the contrary) made me utterly indifferent. I refrain from taking any action because it is no longer good for me or others. By necessity, this state of innocence allows me to enjoy surrendering to my natural desires without pangs of conscience. Perhaps I am going too far, for I am ashamed of even harmless kindness. However, since I have concluded that these circumstances do not show

The Wanderer

me the events as they are, I refrain from passing judgment on what they show. Whatever deceptive forms are given to the factors that lead to any behavior, there is enough left in my thinking to convince me that they are deceptive.

It is as if fate had set its first snare as a child and was accustomed to fall into the next; I am a born believer in anything and everything; I was not deceived in this until I was forty. Suddenly plunged into a completely different environment, I unknowingly got used to a thousand different wardrobes; Twenty years of experience was enough or not enough to see what happened to me. I went from one extreme to the other when I came to the conclusion that your actions towards me were nothing but excuses and lies. Once a man goes out of his natural state; nothing can hold him back anymore. From then on, I hated people, and my desire to be equal with them in this matter made me so far away from my peers that no other human quality could reach me.

But no matter what they do, this threat will not reach the level of hate. When I think of how people have come under my control and dominated me, I feel really sorry. When I'm unhappy, they 're unhappy, and every time I analyze myself, I judge them to be miserable. Perhaps pride also has an influence on this judgment; I don't have the heart to hate them; I

The Wanderer

81

wouldn't replace them at all. Besides, I love myself too much, I don't love anyone else. Not to love would be to narrow my life, to limit it. In addition, I want to expand to the whole world.

I would rather avoid them than hate them; These things affect me very badly; A thousand and one eyes to me would fully increase this effect; but this discomfort goes away after the cause is gone. When I deal with them, when I am near them, I find myself unwilling; not by thinking. In fact, if I don't see them, they seem to disappear.

Moreover, I do not deal with them only in the aspects that touch me: for in their relations they may interest me as characters in the drama I am watching; They can also give me enthusiasm. To be deprived of the sense of righteousness I must die spiritually; and evil and injustice still drive me mad; Even a sign of kindness that does not show itself to others and is unpleasant to others makes me happy and brings tears to my eyes. But I must see and judge it for myself; because after what happened to me, it would be foolish to accept people's verdict on everything and believe something through someone else's eyes.

If people did not know my face as they do not know my character and morals, I would live happily among them; if I were a stranger, I would enjoy meeting

The Wanderer

82

them; I could love them (as long as they cared about me) if I was free to act according to my mood. I would show them a goodness that embraces the whole world and is free from any interest. But I would not be attached to any of them, without carrying any responsibility, and would do very difficult things for them, as required by their dignity and their own rules.

If I had remained the free, solitary, and unknown man I was born to be, I would have done nothing but good; Because there is no seed of evil in my heart. If I were invisible like God and could do anything, I would be as good and blessed as he is. The nation has set an excellent example through power and liberty; Faithfulness and captivity have produced only evil men. If I had the ring of Gyges, it would save me from bowing down to people and bring them under my rule. I often wondered how I would use that ring when I was daydreaming; the desire to abuse a situation approaches power in such an opportunity; What would I always ask of someone who has the power and ability to fulfill my every desire when I am certain that he cannot deceive me? But this is it: pleasing everyone. Only the happiness of all people can give me eternal satisfaction; and I had nothing to do but participate in securing that happiness. Fair and impartial; Being a good man without weakness, I avoided both blind unbelief and intense hatred: seeing men as they were, and easily understanding their secret thoughts, I found among them even those

The Wanderer

83

worthy of my love; And among those same people there were few who were pitied and hated for their evil, because they wanted to harm others and knew that they would harm themselves. With the joy of this, maybe I will have a childhood of creating some miracles. But as I had no personal interest, and desired nothing more than to conform to my natural state, I would have given a thousand different judgments, mingled with mercy and compassion, for a few very severe ones. Determined to obey God's commandments (as far as I could), I would work wonders with the wonder of the golden myth, wiser and more useful than St. Medart's tomb. There is a power in wandering unseen wherever I please, in being unable to control myself: who knows where I would be dragged if I were to take such a path! To hope that I will not be tempted by such honors, and that reason and understanding will prevent me from going too far, is to know neither the character of man nor myself; In short, if I could believe myself in any other situation, I could not believe myself in this situation. Those who rise above men by their power must be above the weaknesses of man: otherwise this great power would not lift him up like himself; on the contrary, he even lowers the level of his own personality, which he would have maintained if he had remained on the level of everyone else.

Well, after considering it, I think it's best if he throws away my magic ring before he makes me a child.

The Wanderer

84

People insist on seeing me differently than I am; if by looking at me their roots of cruelty are stirred, then one should avoid being seen by them, but one should not get lost among them; It's up to them to avoid me, to hide in their closets, to avoid the sun. As for me, if they have strength to see me, well; but they cannot see: instead of me they see Jean-Jacques, whom they have created according to their own hearts to hate. It is therefore a mistake to sympathize with the form and style in which they see me; I shouldn't care about them; because what they see is not me. The conclusion I draw from these considerations is that I have never been fit for public life, where everything is heavy, duty, and necessity, and that I cannot bear the obligations of those who want to live with people, because of my inflexible nature. to accept. If I act freely, I am a good man and do only good; but when I hear the yoke of both necessity and men, I become temperamental and rebellious; then I am useless. If I can't do what I want, I won't go no matter what; however, being a decent person, I will not comply with this request either. I refrain from trying: because I am weak only from trying; My power is entirely negative, and all my sins come not from failure to do something, but from forgetting it. I have always believed that freedom for man is not to do what he wants, not to do what he does not want. This is the freedom that I have always affirmed and believed in, and which has caused my contemporaries to hate me the most. Because they are proactive, active and

The Wanderer

85

passionate; they hate liberty for the sake of others, and do not want it for themselves; allows them to periodically fulfill their wishes, or rather, to dominate the will of others like them; All their lives they force themselves to do what pleases them, but their eagerness to command others does not forget to condemn them to all conditions of servitude. Their crime was not to remove me from society as a useless element, but to ostracize me as a dangerous individual. I will say frankly that I have little good; I have never done evil willingly, and I doubt if anyone has done less evil than I have. A

The Wanderer

86
The Seventh Journey

I feel that the story of my long-running fantasies is over, even though it has just begun. There is another pastime that takes its place and keeps me busy, which keeps me from daydreaming. I take pleasure in this, and I laugh at myself when I think of my pleasure; but if I continue to have that pleasure, I have no hope but to conform to my character in all respects without hindrance in my present state. I can't decide my luck; all my tendencies are innocent; Especially now that I disregard the judgments of men, this is what reason wants me to do, whether in private or in public, obeying no law but my own pleasure, doing as I please, knowing no other measure than measure. whatever force. Here I turned to dry grass as a food and botany as a hobby. When I received my first education from Dr. Ivernois in Switzerland, I was quite old, and had collected enough herbs in my travels to know about plants; but after I was over sixty years of age, and settled in Paris, I could no longer go hunting in the high grass; moreover, as I had no other time to correct what I had written, I gave up this amusement, which was no longer necessary; yes, I sold my books with my collection; While walking around Paris, I enjoyed seeing the occasional plant I came across. Even the simplest information I receive fades away faster than this interval can be recorded in my memory.

The Wanderer

87

I fell in love. To weed with a fever worse than I felt on the first day. I had the clever idea that I had memorized Murray's Regnum Vegetabile and knew every known plant on earth. As I could not afford to buy books on botany, I began to copy what I got, and decided to make a richer collection than before. If I hope to collect all the plants of the seas and the Alps, all the Indian trees, I begin, on the contrary, with the cheap and easy burrage, chrysanthemums, mouse-ears, and winged grasses; The pedant picks grass even from my bird cages, and the tiniest blade of grass is before him: "Here's another plant!" he shouts. I say.

I'm not trying to justify my decision to follow my passion; I consider my decision reasonable, because I consider it a form of virtue in my present state to do what interests me: it is the only way to prevent the growth of hatred and revenge in my heart; In fact, it takes a character free from all anger and violence to take any comfort in the situation I find myself in. Thus I have avenged those who have treated me unkindly, and I cannot punish them with so great a punishment as to be happy in spite of themselves.

Yes, of course, reason and reason compel me to submit to every volition that attracts me and nothing prevents me from submitting; but they do not teach me why this tendency appeals to me, when in my old days I was demented and useless, and lost in memory

The Wanderer

88

and vitality, and took pleasure in the acquisition of useless, fruitless, and empty knowledge. like a student. However, this is a surprise I want to explain. If it is well lit, it will shed new light on the self-awareness that I have given my last free time to.

Sometimes I thought very deeply; but as I liked so little, I almost always thought reluctantly and forcefully. The thought makes me tired and sad; imagination takes away my tiredness and cheers me up. Thinking has always been a difficult and unpleasant profession for me. My imaginations sometimes lead to reflections; but my thoughts often turn into fantasy, and during diversion my soul travels on the wings of my imagination with an ecstasy beyond the universe and any pleasure. As I had tasted this pleasure in its purest form, the other profession seemed to me distasteful; but my sweet dreams, plunged into summer life by external factors, experienced a period of indolence and indolence, when I felt the weariness of the mind, the discomfort of a dark dignity. After a while, when I had to deal with this sad situation involuntarily, I rarely had access to the things I loved that made me the happiest person in fifty years of unemployment. a waste of time instead of promotion and glory.

Moreover, my imagination, alarmed by my sufferings, now turned all its work in that direction to these

The Wanderer

fantasies, and I feared that my sorrows would finally overwhelm me with their burden. I found myself in such a situation that, with a peculiar instinct, I stopped my imagination and began to pay attention to the things around me (for the first time) and began to study the details that I saw before the general appearance of nature. right now.

Trees, saplings, plants are the decoration and clothing of the world. There is nothing sadder than the sight of a bare and bald country; Because he has nothing but stones, mud and sand in his eyes; And the place where nature is alive, dressed in wedding clothes, water flows around, and birds sing, shows people a pleasant life in harmony with nature, a world full of beauty, a world where the eyes and heart do not get tired.

The more sensitive the contemplative, the more ecstatic he is in harmony. Then he sinks into a deep and sweet dream; and he seems to be intoxicated by this beautiful harmony in which he recognizes himself. From that moment on, he can't separate small things and sees everything only as a "whole". He needs an extraordinary story that engages his thinking and imagination so that he can think through the parts of the universe he is trying to fully embrace.

In truth, it was a natural occurrence as I reveled in the agony of my slow collapse, trying to hold on to the

The Wanderer

remnants of my fading warmth. I could not bear to think because I was afraid of repeating my fate, so I wandered through forests and mountains. My anxiety-free imagination made my habits light but pleasant to the things around me. It was impossible not to pay attention to these things, sometimes to one, sometimes to another, and to dwell more on several quite different subjects.

I enjoyed this pleasure of my eyes, I rested and comforted, a narcotic in unhappiness. The nature of the objects helps make this pastime more enjoyable. Sweet scents, vibrant colors, and elegant shapes seem to compete with each other for our attention. To indulge in such sweet feelings, one must love only pleasure; If not all understand, it is because some are insensible, and many are preoccupied with other thoughts and focus on what is distracting them.

There is another point that is effective in removing "taste" owners from the plant world, where the tradition of treating plants only as medicine. Theophrastus saw another; it is for this reason that this philosopher can be considered the greatest botanist of antiquity. That is why it is recognized among us. But the science of medicine, thanks to a man named Dioscorides, who collected many medicinal formulas, took possession of plants and made them possess nothing but properties which they

The Wanderer

did not possess, but which were supposed to possess one or another. The appearance of plants cannot be ignored on its own behalf. Those who spend their lives in the pedantic classification of crustaceans deride botany as a useless subject unless supplemented by other sciences; for liars, those who receive judgment from others, should not cease to observe the nature that does not lie, considering that they are experts and authoritative. Stand in a flowery meadow and look at the flowers: those who see you, mistaking you for a surgeon's apprentice, ask for medicine for their children's baldness, men's scabies, and horse cock.

If this bad custom has somewhat disappeared in other countries, especially in England, it is owing to Linas, who rescued botany from the schools of pharmacy, and owed more or less to natural history and economics. However, this science remained so primitive in France, a gentleman's world, that an elegant man from Paris saw a garden in London full of rare trees and plants and said, "Oh, what a beautiful apothecary's garden!!" he shouted. According to this account, our father Adam should be counted as the first pharmacist: Because in terms of plants, it is impossible to imagine a garden richer than the gardens of paradise.

The Wanderer

92

These medicinal considerations, I think, are not peculiar to the popularization of herbalism; they spoil the enamel of the lawns, wither the flowers, spoil the coolness of the trees, and sink the green and shade into insignificance; This elegant and charming look is not for those who want to conquer everything in one go. The crown worn by shepherd girls is not made of tenkey grass.

All these drugstore products didn't ruin my country look at all; because it was far from the water of the lake. Looking carefully at the countryside, the vineyards, the woods, and the people who lived in them, I often thought of the plants as the stores of food which nature gave to man and beast: but it never occurred to me to seek medicine or cures. there. I don't see anything in any of these products that calls for such use; If nature wanted us to benefit from them, it would have given us plants to eat as well. Moreover, the pleasure I felt while walking through the trees; I feel that plants are poisonous because they suggest the weakness of the human body, reminding me of malaria, sand sickness, palsy, dropsy. However, I do not deny the good qualities that I think plants have; but I will say that if we really consider the virtues, the illnesses of the sick are no more than a joke; for there is not one of the many diseases that men mislead, and there are twenty kinds of herbs that can be cured from its roots.

The Wanderer

93

I have never accepted this concept of looking at everything for our material well-being, looking everywhere for benefit or medicine, and indifferent to nature if not for illness. I feel that I am very different from other people in this respect. Every anxiety that touches my needs saddens me, distorts my thoughts; So much so that I have enjoyed the work of my brain only by denigrating my own interests. Here, if I believe in medicine and its remedies to be pleasant, I cannot take pleasure in dealing with them, in pure and aimless contemplation of nature; As long as I feel that my body is connected to it, my soul cannot rise above nature. The truth is, while I've never had much faith in medicine, I've trusted some of the doctors I love and respect so much that I've let them run my cage of life as they please. Fifteen years of experience have taught me many lessons to my detriment; Now I have returned to my former health only by obeying the law of nature, and if they have no other claims than me, why is it surprising that the doctors are hostile to me? I am living proof of the emptiness of their art and the futility of treating them.

No, nothing that can be called personal, which concerns my (soul's) interests, can really occupy my soul. Only in moments of self-forgetfulness do I drift into sweet dreams. I feel an indescribable spiritual ecstasy, melting among people and becoming one with all nature. When men were my brothers and sisters, I could begin to imagine happiness on earth;

The Wanderer

94

since these thoughts belong to the "whole," I could be happy with everyone's happiness; Ever since I saw my brothers seek their happiness in my devotion, my heart has embraced the idea of a special happiness that belongs only to me. That's when I had to run away so that I wouldn't hate them, I tried to protect them from the attacks of their children, and I took refuge with our common mother. Alone, or more precisely, I ran away from social life and became an anti-human person; For even the most terrible loneliness seems to me preferable to nothing but deceit and enmity, and the attention of the wicked.

In spite of all this, I cannot close my eyelids completely, in spite of all this, I have to refrain from thinking, for fear of bringing my own destruction against my will; for my soul, in spite of its hesitation, desires to extend its existence and sensibility to other creatures; moreover, I could not dive into the vast ocean of nature as before; for my enfeebled and languishing habits find no concrete and immutable subjects to cling to, and my old soul has no power to swim in the tangled sea of ecstasy. My thoughts are now nothing more than affective events, and their scope does not extend beyond the objects around me.

I avoid people, seek solitude, and being a lively character who no longer works or thinks, but keeps me from a sad and lethargic indifference, I become

The Wanderer

interested in the things around me. And out of natural instinct, I chose the best among them. There is no beauty or beauty in the mines: these riches hidden in the earth seem to be overlooked in order not to exercise the greed of men; they are there as a reserve, they are there to compensate for the riches that are more available and more real, and the worse they get, the less happy they are. This is when people call upon industry for help in this difficult business to find hope; stirs the soil; When he knows from the depths to harm his life or health, he looks for the good that should exist instead of the real benefits that the soil itself gives. They shun the sun and the day they are not worthy to see; bury themselves alive: they are right, because they do not deserve to live in the light. There, hearths, rocks, craftsmen, ovens, a whole hill, hammer, smoke, bullets replace the sweet scenes of village life and work. The pale faces of the unfortunate people living in the poisonous atmosphere of the mines, the blacksmiths, the ugly demons: these are the scenes of the mines, the green and flowers in the heart of the earth, which change depending on the presence of the earth. blue sky, shepherds in love and brave farmers!

It's easy to say that it's easy to pretend to be a naturalist by scattering sand and stones, piling them in your pocket and cabinet. However, most of these "collectors" are rich, ignorant people who just want to enjoy showing off. One must be a chemist or naturalist

The Wanderer

to benefit from mineral exploration; perform complex and expensive experiments; he has to work in laboratories, risking his health and sometimes his life, spending a lot of time and money working on coals, rabbits, crucibles, furnaces, in the midst of suffocating fumes and fumes. This exhausting and tedious effort often results in selfishness rather than knowledge. Indeed, even the worst chemist thinks he understands all the great operations of nature, having made an accidental invention or two in his field.

The animal world is closer to us and more worthy of study. But isn't their education accompanied by many difficulties and fatigue? How a single person, who does not expect help from anyone in entertainment and work, observes, interprets and studies the birds in the air, the fish in the water, the quadrupeds that are lighter than the wind and stronger than humans, and they are not ready. Come to me to study, I don't want to follow them. Thus, I have only snails, worms, and flies within my reach; and I spend my life panting after butterflies, pinning poor bugs, and cutting up rats or dead animals. Without doing this work, animal research is futile; The classification of animals and the difference between the various genera and species can only be learned through dissection and study. He must have aviaries, fish-ponds, and live animals, to be able to examine them as to their habits and habits; I have to keep them with me one way or another; But I don't have the ability, the will, or the strength to

The Wanderer

follow them when they are free. Therefore, they should be treated as corpses, dismembered, deboned, pierced; what a horrible sight the cutting room is; rotting corpses, bare flesh, loathsome entrails, loathsome skeletons; poisonous air! I swear, Jean-Jacques will not seek his will there!

Bright flowers, enamel meadows, cool shadows, streams, trees, green trees; Come, cleanse my imagination polluted by these abominations! My soul, no longer capable of great actions, is moved only by sensible things: I have nothing but "sense," and only then can I feel pain or pleasure. Attracted to the sweet things around me, I see, think, compare, and finally learn to classify them; So, all of a sudden, I became a botanist just like everyone else who wants to study nature for new and new reasons to love it more and more every day. I don't try to learn anything; now the time has passed. Indeed, I have never seen so much knowledge contributes to the happiness of life; but I look for sweet and simple pastimes which I can enjoy without difficulty, and which make me forget my ruins. wandering lazily from herb to herb, sapling to sapling, examining them, comparing their various features, seeing their differences and relationships; No trouble is needed to trace the origin of plants, to observe the changes in those living machines, to search for the general laws to which they are subject, and sometimes with success, to investigate the causes and purposes of the appearance of their various

The Wanderer

species. to admire and appreciate the structures and the hands that give me pleasure from them.

If plants are scattered over the earth as abundantly as the stars in the sky, I think it will be an invitation to people to study nature through curiosity and pleasure; the stars are far from us; Accessing and viewing them requires prior knowledge, tools, machinery, and long ladders. Herbology is the work of an unemployed, lazy loner; he needs only a magnifying glass and a toothed stick to observe plants; Wandering freely from one to another, looking at all the flowers with interest, and beginning to feel the law of their formation, he takes deep pleasure in observing them, as if it were an easy but difficult task. The passions of this pleasant profession are felt only when repressed, but make life happy and sweet; but if any personal interest or self-interest joins it, to get a place or to write a book, and try to become a lecturer or writer with the plant, this pleasure is lost and the plants disappear. instruments for our passions; Everyone cares to know, not show what they know, and even the middle of the forest becomes a stage of skill and talent for those who want to admire. Moreover, being limited to research, let alone horticulture, relying only on the methods and methods of research, rather than observing plants in nature, teaches little natural history, apart from proper lighting, creates endless debates. This is where the fame, envy, and hatred that is more widespread

The Wanderer

among botanists than among other scientists comes from. Those scholars destroy their beautiful sciences and take them to cities and academies, where they are destroyed like seedlings plucked from the soil.

My passion for science came from a completely different perspective. It now takes the place of other passions that have left me. I climb mountains and rocks, dive into rivers and trees to avoid people's thoughts and evil intentions as much as possible. When I take refuge in the shade of the forest, I am a free and peaceful person, people seem to forget; protect me from myself, like the absence of my enemies, or the leaves of the trees, like their memories; I don't think my stupid self-cares about me. If my condition, weakness, and needs permit, I will fully immerse myself in the taste I find in this empty fantasy. The lonelier I live, the more I have to try to fill that void; The subject, which my imagination or memory rejects, is replaced by the products of the soil, unforced by men, visible to my eyes from all sides. The joy of picking new plants in the desert is greater than the joy of escaping from those who treat me cruelly; I breathe comfortably in places where there are no traces, as if I am in a shelter where I can escape their hatred.

For the rest of my life, I will remember one day picking grass on Judge Clerk's Mountain, Robiola. I

The Wanderer

100

was alone. I plunged into the hollows of the mountain; My secret place, where I wandered from forest to forest, from rock to stone, was a desert where I had never seen a match. This place is mixed with old and large beech and pine trees. There were only a few gaps around, leading to sheer cliffs or scary cliffs that I couldn't look at before I fell asleep. In the crevices of the mountain white owls, eagles and eagles were hooting. Only rare but familiar little birds calmed the fear of loneliness. There I found a leptophyllous cyclamen, a nidus Avis, a large laser pythium, and other plants, which gave me great pleasure and amusement; but, involuntarily under the strong influence of objects, forgetting plants and their science, I leaned on cushions of lycopodium and moss, and plunged more easily into fancies, and thought that the choppers were in a place where no one could find me, and knew in the world. Soon these fantasies were mixed with a kind of grandeur. I likened myself to the great explorers who discovered deserted islands and thought, "Maybe I'm the first person to get here." I saw myself as a second Christopher Columbus, more or less. As I was swimming in this blood , I heard a rustle in the distance and felt what was happening; I heard; this noise was repeated in the same way, unchanged. Curious and surprised, I got up, and walking through the thickets in the direction of the sound, saw a hosiery factory on a little cliff twenty paces from where I thought I had first seen a human face.

The Wanderer

101

I cannot describe the mixed and conflicting enthusiasm in my heart at this scene. My first feeling was to be glad to be among people where I thought of myself alone, but this feeling was followed faster than lightning by a persistent thought: Even in the Alps, I could not escape it. cruel hands of men determined to torture me. Because I believed that not two people could be found who were not aware of the plan to kill the eloquent Montmollin, which was arranged by factors that came from far away from the factory. However, I did not get rid of this sad thought for a long time, and I laughed when I remembered the childish importance, I had placed on myself and my personality, and how strangely it was punished.

However, who would have thought that a sock factory would be found in a cliff? Switzerland is the only country that mixes wildlife with man-made industry; Its streets, longer than the rue Saint-Antoine, are cut by wooded hills, and the houses are connected by gardens like in England. And so I remembered that we had just assembled with du Perroux, decahenry, Colonel Pori, and Clerc on Mount Chasse Ron, from which the seven lakes were visible.

They said that there was only one house on this mountain; We wouldn't have known if they hadn't told me that the guy who lived there was a well-stocked bookstore. In my opinion, even such a small

The Wanderer

fact makes Switzerland much better known than what travelers write about.

There is another thing similar to this, which does not serve to better know a completely separate nation. While living at Grenoble, Mr. Bouvier, one of his lawyers, and I used to pick hay outside the town; This man felt it his duty to stay away from me, not because he knew or liked botany, but because my personal defenses were broken. One day we were walking along a patch of thorny willow called Isere. I saw the fruits of these little trees; I have tasted; I liked their anger; I ate a lot of these. Monsieur Bouvier stood beside me, silent, but he did not eat like I did. Then one of his friends came and saw me chewing those grains and said, "What are you doing, sir, don't you know that these are poisonous?" - he said. said. "What, is it poisonous?" I was surprised. I cried. "Of course," he said, "everyone knows he won't put it in his mouth." Looking at Mr. Bouvier, he asked: "Why didn't you warn me?" He respectfully answered: - I do not dare to do such a feat, sir! Although I refused to eat nuts, I began to laugh at the humility of the dauphins. I used to think (and still do) that nature's sweet nuts can't harm the body. But it must be said that I did not shut myself up for a whole day; I left work feeling a little anxious. I ate well, slept well; And I awoke the next day in good health, after having swallowed fifteen or twenty of the dangerous hippos has, which, as everyone said at Grenoble, poisoned men, and even

The Wanderer

103

some of them. This adventure seemed so strange to me that I still laugh when I think of the strange shyness of the lawyer Bouvier.

the various impressions I received from the things which attracted my attention, and the thoughts which arose from them, all the events which occurred in them, left in me a resounding feeling. herbs collected in the same places. I will never see those beautiful places, forests, lakes, trees, rocks, mountains, which always fill my heart with feelings; however, it is enough to open my weed and root collection to review myself here. It's a kind of memoir for me.

What connects me to botany is a series of implicit thoughts that bring to mind the thoughts that appeal most to my imagination: meadows, waters, woods, and the solitude, silence, and serenity that can be found in all of these. Thus, I see people's cruelty, hatred, enmity, bad behavior towards me; I forget the evils they have done to me because of the love and sincerity I have shown them, and it seems refreshing to me to be led once more to good and ordinary people, to peaceful homes like those I used to live with. I enjoy it and it still makes me happy, even when a person can suffer.

The Wanderer

104
The eighth journey

When I think about my moods in various situations throughout my life, I am amazed at the disproportion between the positive and negative effects that changes in my destiny have had on me. My brief stints in heaven left no pleasant memories of their lasting impact. And in all the sufferings of my life, I experienced from within myself tender, tender, sweet feelings that healed my sorrowful heart and turned my pain into pleasure. Their beautiful memory lives on, and at the same time they are relieved of their suffering. When I am truly alive, when I enjoy life the most, my feelings seem to gather around my heart because of my happiness; It is a time when the people we think are happy and admired by people, even if they do not have special values, are not scattered in the things that are their only concern.

When everything was fine in my environment and I was happy with it, I surrounded it with love. My soul, which I take pleasure in expressing myself, also covered other subjects. A thousand pleasures took me away from myself, my heart was overwhelmed by many beautiful desires, and I used to forget myself. I would obey things that were foreign to me, and I would feel all the sufferings of human destiny with the excitement of my soul. This tumultuous life did not show a comfortable face for me either inside or

The Wanderer

105

outside. Although she looked happy, I had no feelings, and if I could dwell on that, I would enjoy it. I have never been fully satisfied with myself or anyone else. the noise of the world surprised me, loneliness bored me; I felt the need to change places for a long time, it was not comfortable anywhere. However, everyone loved me, invited me, entertained me; I had no enemies, no haters, no envy. As everyone wanted to serve me, I would have the opportunity to serve them all; Although I have no property, no job, no one to annoy me, no known art, no talent, I enjoyed all of this and believed that no one could be happy with me. What am I missing to be happy? Do not know. But I know I'm not. What is missing to be considered the most miserable of modern men? What people won't do to make it happen. Even in this deplorable condition, I would rather remain in my misery than exchange my wealth and fortune for the happiest of men, and taste theirs. Yes, I remain alone and feed on my essence; but does not run out and is enough for me. Tired of my body, my soul sinks day by day and cannot find the strength to get rid of its old skeleton under this heavy burden.

Unhappiness leads us to think about our destiny; In fact, most people cannot tolerate indulgences. As for me, who find nothing in myself but fault and sin, I give my weakness the ruin that befalls me, I console myself; for there is no evil in my heart of my own free will.

The Wanderer

106

But in my case, it would be foolish not to see that it is dangerous. But I, the gentlest of men, look without pain. And when faced with a situation where no one can see without danger, I remain oblivious to myself.

How did I get to this point? I haven't been so calm in a long time since I accidentally felt the evil surrounding me. I was surprised when I found it; I was shocked by the hypocrisy and betrayal. What pure soul is ready for such suffering? He probably deserves to wait for them. I fell into all the traps set. I got confused with the compass, I got rebellious, angry, stupid. My mind stopped working; I found no light to guide me through the darkness they threw me, no support to keep me alive and to withstand the despair I felt.

How to live comfortably and happily in such a dangerous situation? However, this state still continues, and I live comfortably and happily; I do not think of those who cruelly treat me with sweet flowers and children's games, but I laugh at their incredible self-torture.

How did this change happen? Of course, it is not heard. The first impression was terrible. I thought I was worthy of love, respect, affection and admiration, and I suddenly found myself transformed into a monster unmatched on earth. An entire generation, no doubt, unashamedly, without needing to

The Wanderer

107

understand business, agrees with this strange notion;
Nor can I reach the wisdom of that mysterious change.
I wanted to force my enemies to talk to me; but they
escaped. After a long time of vain grief, I had to rest.
But I still haven't given up hope. And I said to myself:
"Such ignorance cannot be imitated by all mankind,
and such stupidity as knowingly condemns one
person. There are intelligent people who do not agree
with this nonsense, and spirits who hate traitors with
malice. Let's search, maybe I will meet someone at
last, if I find one. , my enemies shall perish. I have
sought in vain. An evil alliance against me has spread
throughout the world, there is no hope; I believe I
shall die in this spiritual exile before I learn its secret.

It was in this sad revolution that, after long toils,
instead of the despair which should have fallen to my
lot, I found happiness in the tranquility of my soul; for
every day of my life, I recall with pleasure the
preceding one, and desire nothing else for the next.

Why does this difference occur? One thing: to learn to
obey without making a sound. I wanted to join a
thousand places, but when everything got out of my
hands and I was left alone, I found my balance again. If
I maintain that balance even when I am squeezed
from all sides, I am not attached to anything, and I
only rely on myself.

The Wanderer

108

When I went against the people with such enthusiasm, I was inadvertently carrying a yoke. We want to be appreciated by those we value and admire; I couldn't care less about people's judgments of me if I could judge at least some of them positively; Although I see that the judgments of the people are often correct, I do not see that justice in this way is anything but accidental, and that the rules on which their opinions are based are derived only from their passions and "needs." their appearance: for though they think rightly, it rests on a bad foundation; For example, by pretending to like a person who is successful in one job, we do not obey the need for justice, but the requirement to appear impartial, and we do not hesitate to criticize the same person in other points.

But after such a long and vain search they all met the cruelest and most senseless sentence from the devil's head, reason drove justice from all minds and all hearts, and a whole generation followed their blind rage. When I realized that I was alone on earth and that my contemporaries were, compared to me, machine beings who could calculate their movements by instinct and the laws of motion, I was alone on earth. None of the purposes or passions I could conceive of, contained in their souls, could explain the situation they had made against me in such a way that I could understand them. Thus, their opinions do not matter to me, they have become nothing more than a

The Wanderer

mass of materialized in various ways, freed from any moral concerns.

No matter what challenges we face, we tend to focus more on intent than results. A shingle falling from the roof hurts us much more, but it does not hurt like a stone thrown by an evil hand; A stone may not hit its target, but it does what it intends to do. Material pain is least felt when falling from a high position; When the poor people find no one to take care of their troubles, they attribute it only to the fate that they themselves have suffered as a rational, open-minded person. A gambler who is upset about being ironed is angry because he doesn't know who he is mad at; He thinks that fate is his enemy, and with this blood that feeds his anger, he burns the enemy he created for himself. A wise man, who feels the blow of blind need only in his own destruction, does not fall into such nonsense; cries in pain, but does not get angry; He feels only the material effects of suffering; No matter how much the blows hurt his body, none of them could reach his heart.

Achieving such a result is not small, but it is still not enough. Discontinuation in this case means not treating the disease after the symptoms are gone. Because this root is not in strangers, but in ourselves. should destroy it there. I felt really good about these when I started to come to my senses. As I tried to

The Wanderer

110

explain to myself what had happened, my mind presented me with many absurd and absurd proofs; therefore, as I could not get to the bottom of it, I perceived that all these causes and means must not be valid in my eyes; to regard all the phases of my destiny as pure "destiny" idiosyncrasies, unattached to purpose or spiritual causes; surrender without rebellion, because it is futile; In spite of the necessity of seeing myself as a man exposed to various influences, I believed that my duty on earth, that I had the power to resist my fortune, should not be wasted by futile resistance to it. So, I said to myself; My mind and heart rely on them, but I still feel them talking to my heart. Where does this word come from? I called; I learned that after challenging people, my dignity defied reason.

Understanding this was not as easy as one might think; for the falsely accused innocent man appears to the pride of his petty ego to be the pure love of justice. However, once the source is found, it is easy to dry it out, or at least redirect it. Self-love is the main factor of solemn souls. Honor, a lot of imagination, can cover the place of approval. But when the trick is revealed and the honor is no longer hidden, he is no longer afraid of it; It's hard to suppress, but it will happen eventually.

The Wanderer

111

I've never cared much about honor. But when I was
living in society, especially when I was a writer, it was
very swollen; It was lighter than mine, maybe lighter
than the others, but still huge. The terrible lessons I
learned quickly shut him down at his core; first he
opposed injustice, then he hated it; He contented
himself by doing good to me, giving up external ties
and comparisons, the advantages (advantages) he
wanted so much for. Then, by reverting to pride form,
it returned to the order of nature, freeing me from
worrying about what others thought.

After that day, I felt rested and found happiness.
Because it is this anxiety that always makes us
unhappy in any situation. If we put it aside and listen
to our mind, we will find solace in the difficulties we
cannot avoid. The ability to avoid dealing with them
and to avoid their most painful effects will make our
mind eliminate these pains to the extent that they do
not immediately enter us. They are nothing to those
who do not think of them. Humiliation, revenge,
attack, injustice and giving up one's rights for the sake
of others are nothing for those who think only of
themselves, do not seek purpose in their pain, and
know that they do not owe their position. the pleasure
of others. I am who I am, no matter how people want
to see me. No matter what they do, no matter their
power, no matter their secret tricks, I will be what I
am. It is true that what they think of me affects my
real condition: the barrier they put between us has

The Wanderer

112

deprived me of any resources to serve my old age and needs ; it also makes money useless, because it is useless for the jobs I need; There was no relationship, communication, cooperation between them and me. I am alone in the crowd; I can only find a way to fix it myself; but, at my age, the solutions I can find in this situation are very poor. The pain is great, great, but it hasn't worked for me since I found a way to resist without getting angry. There are few points defined by real needs; the prudence and imagination which make those points so remarkable; That's why we worry and make ourselves unhappy. As for me, even though I know that I will suffer tomorrow, I will not be sad because I am not suffering today. I don't feel sorry for the trouble I know I have, but the trouble I feel makes it a lot easier. I could die of frost, cold, and hunger alone in my sick bed, and no one would spare me. But what's the matter, I don't spare myself; Am I indifferent to my wealth like others? Is it a small matter, especially at my age, to treat life and death, sickness and health, wealth and poverty, fame and slander with equal indifference? All the old people think about everything, I don't care about anything. Anyway, it doesn't bother me. The secret of this indifference is not in my own mind, but in my enemies, as if they have removed the evil, they have done to me. They have done me such a favor, which is far greater than the favor of protecting me from an accident. Not feeling unhappiness makes me less

The Wanderer

113

afraid of it; And by surrendering myself, I was no longer afraid of him.

This state of mind makes me as carefree as I am in the happiest moments of my life; Except for the brief moments when objects reminded me of my painful worries, my heart was once more drawn to the loves that had drawn me, and my heart was nourished by innate feelings. I enjoy them (as if they were actually alive) with creatures of fantasy who create and share those feelings; But those who created them are living people for Me. I'm not afraid of them letting go or cheating. They live with my downfalls, enough to make me forget my troubles.

Everything seems to bring me back to a new happy and sweet life. I spend three-fourths of my life with interesting and pleasant subjects which nourish my mind and sensibility, or with the children of my imagination, whom I have created and nurtured to my heart's content, or with my happy and happy self alone. I know I have the right. A factor in all of this is my attachment to myself; Otherwise it is not "honor". But the sad moments I have hitherto spent among men whose false sincerity, graceful and pitiful compliments, sweet malice, and playthings are quite different; No matter what I do, no matter what I do, respect reigns. The hatred and enmity I see in their hearts under that rough mold oppresses my heart;

The Wanderer

114

The thought of having been so foolishly caught makes the indignation of honor, which I cannot overcome, even when I feel very well the senselessness of it, more painful. The effort to adjust to these insulting and sarcastic looks is incredible; I have walked through the most crowded places hundreds of times to acclimate myself to my ferocious combat; I too could not resolve anything but failure; As a result of my hard and futile efforts, I became more easily startled, embarrassed, and rebellious than before.

For whatever I do, I must be according to my feelings, and therefore have never escaped their influence; as they are affected, it is impossible that my heart should not feel the same effect. But these temporary mental states, and the emotions that cause them, persist. I am deeply disturbed by the anger of an offended person; But that discomfort goes away with the man's departure. If I don't see it, I don't even think about it. I know he cares for me, but I can't care for him. pain that I do not feel at that moment does not affect me; There is no enemy that I cannot see. I know how this state of mind gives an advantage to those who dominate my wealth.

Let them use their advantage as they please; I'd rather have them torment me without resistance than think about them to avoid their blows.

The Wanderer

115

The only pain in my life is the impact of my feelings on my heart. I can't bear to think about my fate in places where I don't meet anyone. I am happy, content, uninhibited and unchanging. But it is seldom that I fail to notice some blow upon my senses; Even in moments when I'm not thinking about him, a certain behavior, a terrible look in my eyes, an unfortunate person I meet is enough to turn me upside down. What I would do in such a situation is to immediately forget and run away. My heart's sorrow goes with its cause; I'll sleep if I'm alone. What worries me is having another new problem of suffering come my way. This is my only concern; but enough to distract me. I live in the heart of Paris. When I leave the house, I look for solitude with a view of the countryside. But to reach them he has to go so far... Before I breathe easy, I meet a thousand things on the road that hurt my heart, until I reach the corner half the day is spent in anxiety I'm looking for. I'm glad I got to where I was going! The moments when I stand out from the bad people are very sweet, and when I find myself among the trees and the grass, I feel as if I am in paradise, and enjoy myself as if I were the happiest of men.

I remember very well that during my short promotion, the attractions that today seem so attractive, only caused me discomfort. If I was in someone's house in the village, I usually went out alone, walked through the garden or the village, and ran like a thief in the fresh air. But instead of feeling

The Wanderer

116

today's silence, I carried with me the heat of vain thoughts that troubled me in the halls, thinking of the people I left there. The fire of honor, the noise and noise of the world prevented him from hearing the coolness of the forest and disturbed the peace of solitude. Although I fled deep into the woods, the boring crowd watching me covered the entire landscape. I got rid of the love of the society and the poor crowd, and found myself again with all the beauty of nature.

Seeing that it was impossible to curb the tendencies over which my will could not dominate, I thus ceased my efforts. With each blow, I let go of my anger and rebellion, I let go of the nature that at first could not afford to be happy; I just try to neutralize its effects. Flaming eyes, flushed face, shaking organs, suffocating heartbeat - these are all bodily functions that we cannot solve with the mind. But after allowing nature to take its course, man can overcome his ego and come to himself. At first, I failed, then I succeeded. Abandoning my strength in vain resistance, I turn to the possibility of overcoming it; for the mind speaks when it listens. What a? Did I say the right thing? It is a mistake to credit him with victory; for he has no share in the victory. Everything is born of an unstable nature that sways in a strong wind and settles down when the wind stops. The passionate side of that character that annoys me; Calming is the empty side. I surrender to all the challenges I face; any conflict

The Wanderer

causes me to have a short but very intense behavior. When the conflict ends, so does this behavior; Emotions that come from things outside of me cannot live in me. By the accidents of fate, the schemes of men cannot affect the man thus created; In order for passions to impress me constantly, they must be renewed from moment to moment. Because the briefest pause brings me back to myself. When people dominate my sensibilities, I am the person they want; but, for a while, when I have the opportunity, I will be as nature wills me; no matter what they say, this is my permanent state. I told him before. The evil of men does not touch me; What scares me is the evil they will do. However, I laugh at their initial scheme, I don't believe they can cause me permanent pain, and I enjoy myself in spite of them.

The Wanderer

118
Ninth Trip

Happiness is an unstructured, permanent state of mind for humans; Everything in this world shows indecision. Everything around us changes. We ourselves change, and no one can be sure that what they love today will be loved tomorrow. Thus, our assumptions about happiness in this world are always a gross fantasy. If we find peace of mind, let us enjoy it; let us not pass over our sins; but even thinking about tying it up is crazy. I saw few, perhaps none, who were happy; But he often meets people with pure hearts. This is one of my favorite topics. I think it's the result of my love taking over my emotions. My happiness has no outward appearance; To discover it, you need to be able to see what is in the heart of a happy person. However, satisfaction can be understood from the eyes, attitude, tone and voice, and seems to be transmitted to those who understand. Is there any sweeter pleasure than to see the people of a whole country rejoicing on a holiday, and to see all hearts open under the rays of happiness passing fast and strong through the clouds of life?

Three days later, BP, out of his usual generosity, sent me B. showed d'Alembert's "The Praise of Madame Geoff Rin." Before he began to study, he long mocked the ridiculous novelties of the work, and the foolish things it uttered; He was still laughing when he

The Wanderer

119

started reading. I listened with such eagerness that it subsided; He stopped laughing when he saw that I was not laughing. The longest and most admired part of this piece was about Mrs. Geoffrey's delight in watching the children and making them talk. The author says that this tendency shows good character, accuses those who have no appetite as having bad character, and writes that if the thoughts of murderers are investigated, it will be found that none of them like children. Such an argument had a surprising effect on why it was made. Is it really his turn? Is there a place where torture and killing are mentioned while praising a respectable woman? I easily understood the reasons for this abominable display, and after BP had finished reading the work I noted the good points, adding that the author felt more hate than friendship in his heart when he wrote it.

The next day, the weather was cold but beautiful, so I went to the area where the Military Academy is located. I was hoping to find some newly hatched algae there. On my way I remembered the previous day and d'Alembert's letter; I thought that the passage added as a digression to the article was not placed without purpose, suffice it to say that they hid everything, and for what purpose they brought that book. I sent my children to an orphanage; It was enough to make me look like a bad father, and naturally I hated children. As I read these chain

The Wanderer

120

results, I was amazed at the ability of the human mind to turn white into black. Because I don't think so many children have enjoyed playing together as much as I have. Whether on the street or while walking, I stop and look at children's games with an interest that I don't see from others. An hour before BP's arrival, I was visited by the two youngest children of the landlord du Susui. The eldest was seven years old. They showed me so much love, I hugged them so tenderly, and despite the age difference between us, it seemed that these children really liked me. I'm glad they didn't worry because of my age. Especially the little one was so kind to me that I fell in love with him more than anything else, and when they left I was as sad as my children.

I understand that the fact that I sent my children to an orphanage is a little exaggeration and is being portrayed as a "traitorous father who does not love children". However, the main reason I came to such a decision was the fear that those children would not be protected in other ways , and that we would face a more terrible fate. I was not in a position to educate them; if I were indifferent to their future, I would leave my children with their mother or their mother's family, who could not bring them up; the other would turn them into monsters. Even thinking about it makes my heart tremble. Muhammadi Sayyid's position is nothing compared to his attitude towards me. In fact, the snares he later set for me on this topic

The Wanderer

amply confirmed the existence of such an opinion. Indeed, at that time I was far from foreseeing such terrible schemes; but knowing that the worst education for my children would be in an orphanage, I put them there. If I had to start again, this time I would start again without hesitation. I also know that I would not have been a more loving father if nature had been helped by habits.

If I have more or less success in getting to know the human soul, it is because of the pleasure I get from watching and observing children. The same pleasure prevented me from expanding my knowledge in my youth; because I enjoy playing with children so much that I never thought to check them out. But when I saw them startled at my wrinkled face in old age, I was afraid to disturb them this time. I preferred to deprive myself of their pleasure, rather than spoil theirs; Now I find solace in his plays, observing the instinctive and realistic behavior of nature, and denying myself a pleasure which none of our scholars can comprehend. I have said in my articles that the importance I attach to these studies shows that I enjoy doing them. No one on earth believes that "Heloise" and "Emil" will be the work of a person who does not love children.

I have always lacked perceptiveness and expressiveness; Especially since my accidents, my

The Wanderer

122

head and tongue have become completely useless. Thoughts and words seem to escape me; however, nothing requires more understanding and speaking skills than talking to children. What adds to my incompetence in this matter is the importance and value placed on something that is considered trivial by someone who is supposed to be writing because the audience is paying attention and writing specifically for children. I was so shocked by my own awkwardness and incompetence that I would rather be in front of an Asian monarch than an outspoken child.

There is another reason that keeps me away from them today. Even though I have watched them with the same pleasure since I destroyed them, the old me is gone. Children don't like getting old; The sight of weakened nature is very ugly in their eyes. Their disgust enters me; I stop petting them rather than squeezing them or being disgusted. However, this motive, on which truly loving souls depend, is not valid for our male and female doctors. It doesn't matter if the kids don't like Mrs. Geoffrey; if only he loved them! But this kind of love is not for me; unrequited love has no price; I'm not in a position to open a little boy's heart with mine right now. I would be very happy if I could be again; True, I realized this from the pleasure I felt yesterday morning in petting Sussi's children. Because while the maid was doing

The Wanderer

123

my work, the boys came to me with smiling faces and did not get tired of me.

Ah, if I could caress for a few minutes more (albeit a little child) with a pure gesture from the heart, and still feel the joy and pleasure of being with me in someone's eyes, what pains and sorrows this brief but sweet lightness of heart would make Me forget! I do not look to animals for the kindness that people have never shown me. There are few examples that I can bear, but so great in their memory; here is something I would almost forget if I were otherwise; The impression he made on me shows all my love:

Two years ago, I expanded more and more into new regions of France; I then turned left and passed through the village of Cleanout, intending to explore Montmartre. As I wandered about looking nowhere, I suddenly felt someone hug my knee; it was a five-six-year-old boy who hugged me with all his strength; She looked at me with such a sweet, sincere face that my heart was filled with enthusiasm. "Mine would be the same," I said to myself. I hugged and kissed the boy and continued on my way. As I walked, I felt a shortcoming; a new need tempted me to return; I felt sorry for the rude separation from the boy, and thought that there was a certain beauty in his inexplicable behavior that could not be underestimated. Finally, I couldn't stand it and went

The Wanderer

124

back; I approached the boy and kissed him again; The man who sold the bread of Nanterre was passing by at this time; I gave money to buy. Then I started talking. I asked if he had a father. He was a cooper; he was there; showed; I left the boy and was about to head towards him, when I saw a dark-faced man coming ahead of me, who looked like one of the spies. Cooper heard someone whispering something in his ear and looked at me with evil eyes.

When I saw this, I immediately got scared and left faster than I went to the boy and his father, I was depressed. But how often has this enthusiasm been rekindled? I passed by Cleanout several times to see the boy; but I did not see him or his father. At last, from this accident, there remained a lively recollection, mingled with a strange indolence and sadness, like any enthusiasm that occasionally pierced my heart.

But everything can be replaced by something else; my pleasures are few and short, but if they were more, I should not enjoy them so much; I feed them with memories. If they were short, that is, not mixed with foreign elements, perhaps I would be happier than I have ever been. A man in the highest degree of despair thinks himself rich with little: a beggar who finds the lowest coin is happier than a rich man who finds a sack of gold. Those who see the effect on my

The Wanderer

125

soul of such a small pleasure, which I miss in the eyes of my enemies, laugh. I had an excellent taste four or five years ago; I remember with satisfaction that I absorbed it.

One Sunday, my wife and I went to My lot Gate for dinner. After dinner we passed through the forest of Boulogne and arrived at Miette. There we sat in the shade, waiting for the sun to set; We wanted to go back home comfortably through Passi. About twenty little girls came to us, at the head of which was a nun-like woman; some sat, some played. While they were playing, the halachic passed by because of the drummer. I saw girls coveting the halwa; Among them, I think two or three girls with money asked for permission to do the intention. While the priestess was thinking and objecting, I called the halwa chef and said: "Let all these girls do their bidding, I have their money!" I spoke. I spoke. This word caused so much joy that it would be worth it if I donated all my property to them.

Seeing that they had gathered in a chaotic manner, with the permission of the nuns, I lined them up and let them pass one by one. There would be no discontent among them, for there was no empty number, and even for those who had nothing, at least one halwa would fall; And to make the entertainment fun, I secretly warned the halwa maker to leave as

The Wanderer

many gifts as possible and told him that I would pay the difference. So, about a hundred halwa came out; and each of the girls got one; for on this occasion, I showed no indulgence; I didn't want to create a bias and sloppiness that would cause resentment. My wife told those who earn a lot to share it with their friends; Thus, everyone's share was equal, and the joy was shared.

Fearing that he would be proud and reject it, I also begged the nun to make an intention; he received graciously, and took back his will, and received his portion without feigning. That's why I was satisfied with the woman; It showed much more delicacy than fake delicacy, which I liked. During this behavior, a fight broke out and they wanted me to judge. These little girls defending their cause in front of me allowed me to see that, although none of them were beautiful, they made me forget their beauty and their ugliness.

In the end, we parted very happy with each other. That day was one of my best memories. Entertainment is not very expensive; the maximum cost is thirty sums; With this money I bought a hundred francs of joy. Indeed, entertainment is not about money; moreover, he prefers a copper coin to a gold coin. I came several times at the same hour to see those children again; but I never saw them again.

The Wanderer

127

This reminds me of another more or less similar game; but it was before. I had sad days when I had to drop in among the rich and the summer people and participate in their miserable pleasures. I stayed at Chevrette during the host's holidays. The whole family gathered. Everything was done to make the celebration very bright; stage plays were played, feasts were given, firecrackers were fired. There was no time to breathe; it was not entertainment, but some sort of consolation. After dinner we went for a walk on the highway; something like a fair was organized there. It was a dance; Gentlemen danced with peasant women, heartily; but the ladies didn't mind. Sour bread was also sold. A young man among us took these loaves and threw them to the people. The kicking, fighting, and fighting of the riot was so good that everyone contributed to the fun. So, the bread flew, the boys and girls ran, and there was silence. This scene delighted the audience. Even if I didn't like them like they did, I seemed to delight in the senseless modesty, like everyone else. But I got tired of emptying my wallet to tempt those people to oppress each other, so I walked off and wandered around the fair. I saw five or six Savalas surrounding a little girl who was standing next to a dozen or more skinny apples. They wanted to save the girl from their apples. But all of them had only two or three sauces, and they could not pay the price of apples with them. I like this situation; I paid for the apples and distributed them to the children. At that moment, I

The Wanderer

128

witnessed an incident that hurt my heart when childhood selfishness mixed with joy and spread to the environment: the audience also joined in that joy; The fact that I provided the joy I shared so cheaply also gave him great appreciation.

Comparing my own pleasures with those from afar, I loved the contrast of rich pastimes, which were nothing but contempt and mockery of pure and natural pleasures. What pleasure would he have in seeing these poor people struggling for a few scraps of mud and trampled bread?

As for me, when I thought of my high pleasure in having such opportunities, I found it more a pleasure to see happy faces than a pleasure. Although such a view pierced my heart, it intrigued me as if it arose from a mere "passion". If I don't see the satisfaction I'm creating (even if I believe I'm giving it), I'm not satisfied. Moreover, it is a pleasure that does not depend on my share, and does not benefit from it: I was always interested in the possibility of seeing happy faces, for example, at holidays. In France, which is supposed to be cheerful, but does not bring joy from entertainment, I have always been deceived in this respect. I used to go to divan taverns a lot to see people dance; but these dances were so shameful, and their manners and manners so lethargic and clumsy, that I was sad instead of happy. But in Geneva and

The Wanderer

129

Switzerland, where laughter is not mixed with impurity or mockery, everyone carries the joy and happiness of the holiday. Love does not come out of ugly scenes there. Wealth does not show its greatness. With the unity of the heart and brotherhood, he invites everyone to cheer. In that fresh air, people who don't know each other meet, mix with each other and enjoy the day. It is enough for me to look at them; Looking at them, I agree with their joy, I come to the conclusion that among such cheerful people, there is no such happy heart as mine.

Although this is only a sensual pleasure, it certainly has a spiritual source; It is clear from this that the face of the same evil people, when I realize that they have succeeded in their evil deeds, I do not like it, I rebel. My heart rejoices only in pure joys. The stone is sad (even if it doesn't touch me) it's a cruel pastime. All these symptoms are, of course, not alike, as they arise from different causes; but they are all signs of joy, and their perceptible difference is not so strong as the reactions they produce in me.

I hear better for signs of pain and sorrow; So much so that I am more excited in front of them than I am in them. My imagination, inflamed with passion, unites me with the sufferer, and often gives me more anxiety than he. I can't bear to see an angry face; Especially when I realize that this bitterness is affecting me... I

The Wanderer

130

can't tell you how much I have spent grumbling and grumbling at servants who reluctantly served me in houses where I was once a dragging idiot. In fact, the servants of those houses always paid me dearly for their master's hospitality. Overwhelmed by all that touched the senses, especially signs of joy or pain, of goodness or hatred, I gave in to these outward impressions and escaped them. A gesture, a sign, a look from someone I don't know is enough to break my mood or ease my pain. I find myself alone; except for loneliness, I am the toy of my environment.

I enjoyed living in a society where I was sincere in everyone's eyes and at least indifferent to those who did not know me. But today, with such efforts being made to publicize me and at the same time hide my true identity, every time I step on the street I am confronted with heart-wrenching issues around me. I run towards the village; I take a deep breath as soon as I see the greens. Is it any wonder that I don't like being alone? I see nothing but hostility in the faces of the people; but nature always smiles at me.

But to be honest, I like living among people who don't know me yet. But now it was pleasure that denied me. A few years ago, I used to go through the village and see the farmers repairing their swamps and the women sitting in front of their doors with their children.

The Wanderer

131

There was something emotional about it. I used to watch the actions and behavior of those gullible people and sigh, not knowing why. I wonder if they saw me enjoying this kind of entertainment and wanted to deprive me of it too? Anyway, it took a lot of effort to introduce myself to everyone, to understand the changes in the faces and looks of the people I met. The same thing happened with disabled people. I am always fascinated by this beautiful institution. I have always looked at old people with love and respect, who can be called "young, brave, agile" like the Spartans.

One of my favorite places was around the Military Academy. There, I met war disabled people who bowed as I passed by, keeping the tradition of military service. This greeting, which I sincerely answered a hundred times, increased my pride and increased my desire to meet them. Since I could not hide anything about myself, I often spoke about the war disabled and how their situation affected me. I realized that I am not a stranger to them, that they know me very well the way people look at me. The greeting was interrupted. Respectful behavior was replaced by stern faces and hostile looks. Since the openness of the chest and the openness of the speech, which were the requirements of their actions, did not allow mocking and lying attitudes, they showed revenge that did not need to be hidden. My pain has reached

The Wanderer

such a level that I appreciate those who do not hide their anger at me.

Since then, I don't like wandering around the disabled area. However, since my feelings for the disabled are not tied to their feelings for me, I will always look up to these brave men who defend their country with respect and interest; but it grieves me that they have so badly responded to my gratitude to them. If I meet a person who somehow does not know what is being said to me, or who is not hostile without knowing me, his polite greeting makes me forget the rudeness of others. In fact, forgetting about all this, I have a relationship only with him, and I think that he has a soul that does not hold grudges like mine. Last year I had the same pleasure when I went for a walk to Swan Island. A poor old war cripple was waiting to cross in a boat. So, I got on and told the boatman to set off. The water was rough; the journey was very long; As usual, I did not speak because I was afraid that we would treat the old soldier badly. But his experienced perspective put me at ease. We talked. He gave the impression of a reasonable and honest person. His clear and gentle demeanor surprised and intrigued me. I understand that they did not introduce me yet and did not give any information about me. Taking advantage of my anonymity, I interviewed for three to five minutes; The pleasure I found in this interview taught me that the cost of the simplest entertainment only rises once every forty years. He was getting

The Wanderer

133

ready to take a penny out of his pocket and was about to get off the boat. I paid the boatman's wages, asking him to put the money in his pocket if he didn't mind. he did not mind; On the contrary, being older than me, he was very happy when I helped him get off the boat. Who would believe that I cried for joy as a child! I was dying to squeeze some sauce into his hand so that he would buy cigarettes; but I couldn't bear it. The same despondency has often hindered me from good works which would open my heart; I cursed my foolishness by refusing them. That day, as I was leaving the old soldier's side, I thought that I was going against my principles by mixing money with pure and useless works, spoiling their nobility, and defiling them with the indifference of interest; This thought comforted me. Help those in need; but let us not interfere with the work of charity and charity in our daily dealings; Let's not poison such a pure resource with the burden of money or trade. They say they get paid for telling the time or giving directions in the Netherlands. Must have been a very dirty people trading in the most mundane human duties.

Only in Europe have I seen hospitality sold for money. Nowhere in Asia is a guest charged. Maybe it's impossible to console, but it's a small thing that says "I'm human, people will entertain me, only civility will welcome me"? If we take care of our heart more than our body, we will easily tolerate small imperfections.

The Wanderer

The Wanderer

135
The tenth journey

It is fifty years since I met Madame de Warrens on Easter Day. He was twenty-eight years old when he was born. I had just turned seventeen, and my self-made, still-developing, but unknown, innate soul was giving new warmth to my heart. While it is not surprising that she should put up with this lively, but mild, shy, but polite young man, it is not so surprising that a very elegant, very slender woman should show me more feelings of affection than I gratefully noticed. But what's even more amazing is that the minute I met him, he defined my entire life and decided my entire life's destiny with the inevitable continuation. My soul, which cannot develop its most valuable talents through construction, has not yet been firmly established. He looked forward to the uniform; but the moment which should have been hastened by that acquaintance did not come so soon as he had hoped; Simplicity, love, and chastity, which was the demand of the education he received, savored for a very long time that delicious but brief mood which lived in one heart. My soul drove me; but as everything was leading me to him, I had to turn to him. This turning point gave a decisive shape to my destiny. Before I met my soulmate, I lived for him and in him. What comfortable and wonderful days we would spend together! We haven't tasted it yet, but it was very short; what happened next! There isn't a day that I don't remember with joy and pleasure the short time

The Wanderer

that I lived without obstacles and difficulties. Like the general who was removed from office under Vespasianus and spent his last days in the village, I can say, "I have spent seventy years on earth, and I have lived seven of them." Without this short and precious time, I could not have decided on my own. For the rest of my life, through my meekness and meekness, I was so drawn by the passions and elevations of others, that I could not determine the share of my own will in my actions, for in such a tempestuous life I obey all. However, thanks to the love of a pretty, graceful woman, I was able to do what I wanted and get what I wanted during those few years, and with her example and lessons, I was able to spend my free time in good shape. my still simple and young soul suited him best and has kept him ever since. The pleasure of solitude, of reckoning with myself, appeared in my heart along with the feelings of love created to nurture it. Noise annoys and suffocates them, and silence enlivens them. To love I must listen to myself. I urged "my mother" to the village. They took refuge in the house on the side of the cliff; but we lived there for four or five years, a century of happiness that made me forget my terrible happiness today. I was looking for a friend after my heart; this friend was him. I wanted to live in the village and I got my wish. I would not tolerate being dependent on anyone; here I was free; I was not just free: because I was bound to my love and did what I wanted. My time was always reserved either for my

The Wanderer

137

love or for the work of my country. I don't want such a wonderful life. My only fear is that it won't last long. If our situation is unnatural, it shows that fear is fundamental. That's why I started looking for ways to eliminate anxiety and prevent its consequences. Believing a wealth of ingenuity and skill to be the surest antidote to indulgence, I resolved to devote all my leisure to this purpose, to prepare myself for a day (if possible). his.

-END-

The Wanderer

www.ingramcontent.com/pod-product-compliance
Lightning Source LLC
Chambersburg PA
CBHW061602250726

48657CB00017B/1435